# CONTEMPORARY AMERICAN
# doll artists
## AND THEIR DOLLS

kathryn
witt

## COLLECTOR BOOKS
*A Division of Schroeder Publishing Co., Inc.*

FRONT COVER: **Alissa** by Monica Reo, photo by Dick Dettloff, $4,800.00 (see page 41 for information); **Blue Ice Faerie**, by Kim Jelley, photo by Kim Jelley. Blue Ice Faerie is pure wintry magic. About to take flight with her magical (and removable) ice wings, she is hand-sculpted of a Premo/Cernit polymer clay over armature and painted with the finest artist paints. Including her wingspan, she measures 6" high by 14" wide and has mesmerizing hand-painted teal blue eyes and pale blue skin. $980.00; **Cocoa** by Anna D. Puchalski, photo by Anna D. Puchalski. Limited Edition Cocoa dolls are approximately 12½" tall, cast in Flumo Ceramic, and are fully jointed with 13 points of articulation. "Clothing is removable and I encourage play and interaction with these dolls (for grown-ups, anyway)." $160.00; **The Golden Faerie** by Marilyn Radzat, photo by Linda Ching. A vision of enchantment personified, The Golden Faerie is hand-sculpted in Prosculpt clay and then burnished in golds and browns and costumed with antique fabric and trim. Like all of the artist's fantasy figures, The Golden Faerie showcases the art of assemblage integral to Marilyn's work. $2,000.00.

BACK COVER: **Hairy Face-The Pioneer Santa** by Mary Masters, photo by Mary Masters. This is a "totally new and different Santa" for the artist. Hairy Face looks like a mountain man and has a great, dimpled smile on his lips. Available in five different cloak colors, Mary says she cannot tell which one she likes the best. "I think if we'd had a Santa Claus 200 years ago, he would have looked just like this pioneer Santa." $90.00; **Kacinda** by Sue Sizemore, photo by Sue Sizemore. With a face constructed of cotton balls under gusseted cloth and wearing a full head of natural, sun-tipped wool hair, 16" Kacinda shows off a choker Sue designed from a flat button that she hand painted with a tiny flower before applying a lacquer finish. She is costumed in a reproduction 1930s cotton dress. $275.00; **Lizzie and Oleanna** by Mary Ellen Frank, photo by Mary Ellen Frank. In Lizzie and Oleanna, Mary Ellen Frank explores the clothing customs of the Alutiiq and Aleut — two non-Eskimo, indigenous peoples from western Alaskan peninsulas and islands. Lizzie's tunic is made of shiny pigskin to suggest sea bird with crow feathers to represent the shiny black cormorant and strips of red leather with white ermine and decorative stitching to separate the rows. Oleanna's coat is made of pine squirrel cut to look like sea otter and sewn in strips with some reversed to take advantage of color variations. Oleanna wears a pair of waterproof Aleut style boots. Lizzie is barefoot, a realistic depiction of the era in which she lived, but her head is covered with a beaded headdress. According to Mary Ellen, the beads would have been traded with Russians for otter skins or weather-resistant clothing made by women. $4,680.00; **The Promise** by Karen Williams Smith, photo by John G. Smith. $3,500.00 (see page 92 for information).

Cover design by Beth Summers
Book design by Heather Warren

COLLECTOR BOOKS
P.O. Box 3009
Paducah, Kentucky 42002-3009

*www.collectorbooks.com*

Copyright © 2004 Kathryn Witt

The current values in this book should be used only as a guide. They are not intended to set prices, which vary from one section of the country to another. Auction prices as well as dealer prices vary greatly and are affected by condition as well as demand. Neither the author nor the publisher assumes responsibility for any losses that might be incurred as a result of consulting this guide.

## Searching For A Publisher?

We are always looking for people knowledgeable within their fields. If you feel that there is a real need for a book on your collectible subject and have a large comprehensive collection, contact Collector Books.

# Contents

# Dedication

*For my mom and dad, Helen and Glenn Lentz, who gave me my first doll and so much more.*

# Acknowledgments

Along the path to creating this book about doll artists and their dolls I encountered many people who offered their insights and assistance, advice, information, and encouragement. I would like to thank Lisa Stroup, a former editor at Collector Books, who had faith in this project from the very beginning and said the kinds of encouraging words every writer loves to hear. I would also like to thank my good friend and very thorough librarian, Anita Owen Carroll, who I've called upon countless times for her expertise. Also on the path was Nayda Rondon, editor of *Dolls Magazine*, who gave me my first doll article assignment, and who demonstrates an admirable level of professionalism and enthusiasm in the business of writing about dolls. I would also like to thank the doll artists who so generously shared their time, their photography sources, and themselves. Finally, special gratitude to the one person without whom this book would not have been possible: John Witt. Thank you each and all.

# About the Author

Kathryn Witt writes for numerous publications in the United States and in the United Kingdom, including many of today's most popular doll magazines. She also writes for a wide variety of travel publications and frequently combines her interests in travel and in dolls during her treks. She is the author of more than 25 books for children, most recently of a series of six graded readers called *Teegan's Travels*.

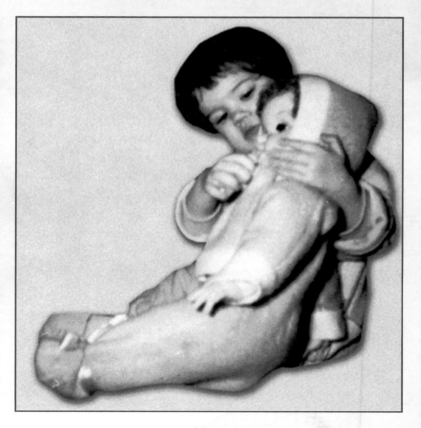

Author Kathyrn Witt, age 2, with her first doll.
Photo by Glenn Lentz

# Foreword

*"We must play the song we came on earth to play.*
*We must not die with our music still in us."*
— *Unknown author*

Author Kathy Witt has impressive credits as a freelance writer with articles on subjects as diverse as travel, parenting, antiques, and quilts. Included among her list of titles and publications are many doll-related subjects that infer a study and understanding of concept and application which implies appreciation and expertise in this complicated art form.

Common among publications about dolls is the singular expertise and/or interest of authors; e.g., period, collecting, teaching, organizations. Few authors have purposely selected a group of artists with intent to showcase the myriad motivations, methods, and materials of present day. Through an insightful blend of profile and technique, Kathy's examples show how the combination of imaginative manipulation of materials and evolving technology affect contemporary doll making.

The book's title, supported by Marilyn Radzat's beguiling fantasy figure, Kim Jelly's ice princess, Anna Puchalski's dark beauty, and Monica Reo's period piece, raises our curiosity. Within, there are no passive expressions in either words or dolls; every page causes a response. The content is consistently pertinent to every person who loves creative effort and, for those seeking information, is nicely sprinkled with tips on method and technique. For authenticity, the credentials of each artist are printed on their introductory pages with prices, media, and affiliations.

The incorporation of an extensive array of media causes one to say, "If you think of it, these artists use it!" From nature's own to manmade, the range of materials is of interest: fabric; air dry, oven baked, and kiln fired clays; wood; composition; resin; wax; glass; crystal; beads; feathers; found objects; even bronze. In addition, themes have been completed by integrating their doll's clothing and accessories into the original process. Appropriately, these additional pieces and methods are included in the discussions.

Without exception, artists I've met have said: "I am compelled." Inexplicably, motivation is tied to inspiration and mandatory to fulfilling the creative urges. To satisfy a universal desire to understand cause and effect, Kathy asked the individuals to share what inspires them to create. Then, under the subtitle, "Wellspring," she introduces each profile with the artist's response. Those reasons, as diverse as the lifestyles and events chronicled herein, establish our sense of the persons.

I guarantee, once this book is in hand, you will be compelled to read every word and enjoy every photograph, and refer to it again and again. The title may indicate present day, yet the book's content will remain timeless and endlessly pleasurable.

Barbara Campbell
Former editor of *Contemporary Doll Collector Magazine, Doll Crafter,* and *Soft Dolls & Animals,*
and Honorary Member of the National Institute of American Doll Artists

# Introduction

*Doll art gets under our skin and into our blood.*
*It speaks vividly to our minds, hearts, and souls.*

So says Michigan doll artist Monica Reo, and doll artists everywhere would agree. Once they pick up that ball of clay or scrap of fabric, they simply cannot put it down. Hours later, a little piece of the artist is rendered in a beautifully transfigured bit of material, a twinkle in its eyes and a story on its lips.

*Contemporary American Doll Artists and Their Dolls* shares the stories that reflect the artistic expressions of 25 doll makers through the dolls they create and the stories behind the creation of the dolls — stories that speak of the artist, her life experience, her sense of wonderment and artistry, and her source of inspiration, her wellspring. It looks at American artists currently working at the craft of doll making, the materials and tools they use, the way they work, and what they bring of themselves to their work.

Although the doll artists are classified into specific categories (i.e. "Healing and Spirituality," "History and Heritage," "Christmastime," "NeedleArts," etc.), many could easily fit into several categories. Gail Lackey is found in the chapter entitled "Wellspring," but with her whimsical children and "weird little men," she could also have a place in "Otherworld" and in the section on "Storybook Creatures and Characters."

Fine art doll maker Karen Williams Smith is featured in the chapter, "September 11," because of her evocative tribute piece, "The Promise," that recalls the youngest victims of the September 11 tragedy, but she could be very comfortably included in "Healing and Spirituality" as well. Karen has sculpted memorials to Anne Frank and to children afflicted with Down Syndrome. She could also be part of the "Wellspring" chapter; her source flow is like a rich spring that bubbles over into many creative streams.

Artist Kim Jelley is also found in the "September 11" chapter. Her Forget-me-not fairy was made to honor the memory of the sister she lost in the World Trade Center collapse, but like Karen Williams Smith, Kim could be in "Healing and Spirituality" because the process of creating this figure was very much a healing one for her. She would also be at home in the book's opening chapter, "History and Heritage." Her Forget-me-not fairy, informed by the lifelong relationship she shared with her only sibling, captures a specific moment in time, recording that moment in all its tragic, horrifying, and ultimately uplifting implications.

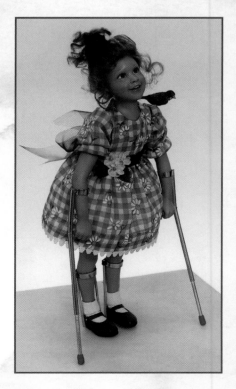

One thing I have learned from writing about doll artists from all over the country and the world — many of whom are featured in this book and whose artistry continues to beguile and beg further exploration — and for a variety of doll publications is that, while each artist has her own niche on the artistic continuum, none of them can be neatly categorized. Each follows her own creative impulse, a journey that begins in the heart. The artists are inspired by many things: colors, fabrics, people, characters, tragedies, triumphs, history. Their work speaks volumes of that which resides in their hearts, their minds, and their spirits.

The doll artists in this book work in all media: clay, cloth, bronze, porcelain, and resin. They come from places all over the United States: small towns, country burgs, sprawling cities, resort destinations. Most were born in the United States; others are naturalized citizens, hailing originally from Japan, Iceland, and the Bahamas. Ranging in age from 28 to 78, all of the artists have been making dolls for at least 10 years and some for as long as 50, yet all of their work is consistently imaginative, never conventional, and always reflective of the artists' unique points of view and cultural experiences.

Putting a value on the dolls in this book is as unique a process as creating them. These doll artists focus on original, one-of-a-kind pieces and pricing is necessarily subjective and extremely personal, and based on many criteria: time, money, and materials invested in the piece; level of complexity; an intrinsic value derived from a special connection the artist feels for the doll; and supply and demand.

Says Gail Lackey: "How do you put a price on something that comes from your soul? It's your baby, and it's the only one in the whole world — never to be another like it!"

Some of the dolls are listed as "in private collection," which means that the doll may have been given as a gift by the artist, created as a commissioned piece whereby the price remains undisclosed at the wishes of the patron, or bought by a celebrity with the understanding the celebrity's name and the price of the piece would remain confidential. Some of the dolls are never sold, but remain in the artist's personal collection permanently, as is the case with doll artist Mary Ellen Lucas who uses her dolls as teaching tools. Regardless, values do increase and the prices listed for the dolls in this book do not necessarily reflect what a similar piece would be sold for today.

Price may vary, but one thing each of these artists shares is her unfettered spirit. The artists are experimental and innovative like Anna Puchalski, who made her own complex system of clay ball bearings; Jamie Williamson, whose museum discovery allowed her to add a fresh, new dimension to her doll vignettes; and Jean Bernard, who likes nothing better than to hide intricate and multifaceted design elements in her sculpting.

They are adaptable like Mary Masters, whose discovery of her grandmother's Skookum doll, a Native American Indian spirit doll, gave her the technology to offer her collectible dolls to many rather than just a few. And they are dedicated, like Jean Lotz, who is busily sculpting new wooden dolls after successive family tragedies sidelined her creative flow.

These doll artists are also constantly evolving, changing and improving their work — never satisfied with their best, but always reaching beyond, to a standard they say they will never achieve because, in doll making, as in life, perfection is an ideal, not an absolute.

(Page 6, top left) Gail Lackey's 16½" tall Marley's Ghost is polymer clay over a wire armature. His clothing is made from antique fabric from the 1800s combined with distressed new fabric. He has hand-painted glass eyes and the requisite, dusty old cobwebs about his attire. $1,950.00.
Photo by Gail Lackey

(Page 6, bottom right) Robin's Dream, an edition limited to just 20 pieces, by Karen Williams Smith is a special earth angel. "Robin is as fresh and open as springtime. She wants to be treated as much as possible like any 'normal' child. She has the same hopes and dreams as other children." The 12" resin doll is valued at $135.00 and is signed and numbered by the artist.
Photo by John G. Smith

(Above) Jean Bernard's deceptively simple chair made of green and gold leaves sits on chair legs that look like twisted tree branches. On closer inspection, one notices that the left leg is actually a dragon's head and the right leg is the dragon's claw. "I love visual surprises. Under the chair seat is what looks like a tree branch but it too is a dragon's body and his tail swoops out the back of the chair looking like a tree branch." Jean textured the entire bottom half of the chair to look like dragon scales, but at a distance it looks like a tree. $185.00.
Photo by Jean Bernard

# Healing and Spirituality

*"Each doll is different, but can still be seen for the beauty of its differences. Dolls can represent people from other countries and teach us about cultures we are not familiar with. We can reach out to a doll of another race for we can see the similarities we share in the common human experience."*

-Marcia Dundore Wolter

Native American Kimberly by Marcia Dundore Wolter. Marcia spent six months working on the solid beading on the yoke of the leather gown and on the tops of the moccasins worn by the 30", porcelain Native American Kimberly. "My daughter-in-law, Becky Wolter, was given the dressed doll for Christmas but she didn't get to take it home until the beading was finished — just in time for her birthday in July!" $695.00.

## Colleen Levitan

Studio .....................Dayton, Ohio
E-mail .....................colleen4dolls@aol.com
Medium...................Polymer clay
Dolls' Price Ranges ..$2,200.00 – $6,500.00
Member..................Dayton, Ohio Painters and Sculptors

### *Wellspring:*

"Faith: Faith in God and faith in the creative process."

### *Clay Keepsakes*

If the miniature bride and groom figures topping the wedding cake are identical versions of the just-married couple, right down to the lacy trim on the bridal veil and the boutonniere on the groom's tux, chances are the cake topper was designed by Ohio portrait doll artist Colleen Levitan.

Colleen's three-dimensional polymer clay cake toppers capture in perfect miniature detail the bride and groom in gown and tuxedo. Following the process she established for working on her portrait dolls, but working with the tiniest of tools (straight pins, needles, and toothpicks), the artist spends untold hours sculpting the wee figures for these "instant heirlooms."

Colleen already had experience in the bridal market sculpting bride and flower girl dolls. She had created a delicate porcelain beauty named Ashley, a wedding belle priced at $1,200.00, and flower girls Caroline and Precious, the latter of which was made for the Home Shopping Network and online site, QVC.

For the cake topper, which can be made for a 6", 7", or 8" base, Colleen requires photographs of the bride's and groom's faces (full face and profile), plus a full-length body shot; photographs of the bridal attire, including the veil, showing drape and detail; and a thorough description of the bouquet. The keepsake can be created for just-marrieds as well as already-marrieds, regardless of how many years it has been since their trek down the aisle. A lead time of three months is necessary in most cases to sculpt the cake toppers.

### *Recreating Picture Perfect Moments*

Colleen Levitan likes to say that she creates memories with her portrait sculptures, but it is actually more accurate to say that she recreates them — and beautifully preserves them in perpetuity.

Colleen's specialty is creating three-dimensional fine art portrait dolls. Her one-of-a-kind pieces, sculpted in polymer clay, are the very embodiment of her subjects' life energy — whether she is creating from a living being or from an assemblage of recent or vintage photographs.

"Being able to capture a very close likeness of a person in a doll is soul-satisfying. I feel a link between myself and the subject. It is almost as if an umbilical cord is attached between us. It is not only a physical connection, but a spiritual one as well."

This connection was doubly in force when Colleen sculpted Gail, her card partner and granddaughter, capturing the little girl's likeness in all its exuberant joy. Gail had been photographed as she played Canasta and her expression, the very antithesis of a poker face, shows her excitement on discovering her great foot of cards. Gail the doll is wearing the play clothes of real-life Gail, cut down to size by Colleen for the 32" sculpt.

Formerly a watercolor portraitist and art teacher, Colleen has been designing portrait or character dolls since the early 1990s, achieving a benchmark verisimilitude distinguished by remarkably expressive faces and body poses. She developed her talent for perfectly capturing a person's face and spirit while designing a series of life-like puppets for a Sarasota, Florida-based non-profit organization called FACE. Her puppets were part of a program to help school-age children become more sensitized to the needs and feelings of children living with a variety of physical disabilities.

"Making these puppets seemed to tap into a natural talent I had for sculpting. I had always had a fascination with dolls. But way before that I was fascinated by faces, various expressions, lines, moods, ages, and especially, the innocence of childhood."

After taking a workshop in doll making, Colleen decided to combine her background in watercolor portraiture with designing original fine art sculptures. Many of her commissions, such as young Phil and Alex, shown garbed in replicas of favorite childhood togs, and toddler Amy, an award-winning piece that recaptures a child's joy of reading her first book, come from a parent or grandparent who wants a doll made of a child or grandchild.

If the child is available, Colleen takes extensive photographs to document every aspect of appearance and proportion; otherwise, she works from existing photographs. Her sculpture brings all of these moments in time, sometimes recent, oftentimes long forgotten (and packed away in attic scrapbooks) back to life. Her dolls have such life-like qualities that the artist will grow attached to them and find it difficult to part with them. She is frequently startled by the realism each doll communicates.

"When I get to the point where I've combined a doll's body parts, that's the moment they come alive to me — so alive in fact that it's almost startling."

The doll maker chalks it up to an uncanny knack, the same one possessed by many police sketch artists, for summoning a person's essence into her fingertips and then molding it into the clay.

"It's because of the connection I am able to establish. You develop a really close relationship with your clients in doll portraiture because they are asking you to sculpt them as they or their children were when they were little or as they are now.

"It's like putting together an intricate puzzle. I take all of the portrait information, gather up all of the pieces of the puzzle, and then recreate that person in the most harmonious and beautiful way that I can while staying true to the original subject matter."

Colleen begins each doll by molding an egg-shaped ball of aluminum

"Real" Gail and doll Gail, a 32" polymer clay portrait doll capturing the little girl as a seven-year-old, sits in a miniature wooden replica of Colleen's own dining room chair that the artist hand painted with pine scrollwork. "Her clothes were cut down from her actual shirt and jeans." $6,500.00.

10

foil which becomes the underlying armature for the doll's head. Next, the eyes are carefully positioned into the foil and framed out with clay. Other features follow: the forehead, brow, nose, cheeks, lips, teeth, and chin.

"The sculpting of the face is the most critical and time-consuming aspect of the process. I work the elements of the face for several days, adjusting and refining the features until I get the most lifelike and expressive likeness possible."

Throughout the process, Colleen is molding, evaluating, and perfecting. She maintains her spiritual connection with her subject right up to the instant she senses that she has perfectly captured a person's physical and spiritual essence, with every idiosyncratic nuance, in a three-dimensional sculpture.

"When I'm working to capture someone's face and spirit, I have an epiphany moment when I know it is exactly that person. I'll hold the sculpt in my hands and be completely aware that God is working with my hands, that He is the one working through me to shape what I'm creating."

Once Colleen is satisfied with the face, she sculpts the back of the head, forming the ears and putting them into position. Arms, legs, hands, and feet are then hand-sculpted, one piece at a time, and a cloth body is made in proportion to the limbs. The dolls average 25" to 32" in size.

The doll is then dressed, sometimes in vintage-wear, oftentimes in garments selected to match clothing worn in a favorite photograph. Colleen designs a stand for each doll as needed and then adds personalizing accessories that can include childhood toys and stuffed animals, books, musical instruments, and chairs — all designed in miniature. Each commission typically takes about eight weeks to complete, depending on the doll's complexity, clothing, and any hand-made accessories.

Polymer clay Sparrow (28") and Asian Baby (14") snuggle in a replica of the real little girl's rocking chair. Sparrow wears an old-fashioned bonnet and overalls. The baby was added later because it just worked. $2,700.00.

Nikki, a young miss bursting with charisma that Colleen spied in a garden store, wears a blue French rose patterned dress with layers upon layers of petticoats. Sparrow, based on a little girl who lives not far from the artist, wears a blue checked bonnet, overalls, and a precocious smile. Perched in a tiny oak rocking chair with her named carved into it, Sparrow clutches her doll, Asian Baby. The doll's doll was made after Colleen saw a picture of a sweet Asian baby in a magazine.

"I had made the baby's face already because the face in the magazine was so cute, so I decided to put a doll together and then put her in Sparrow's arms."

From the commission to the physical connection to the finishing stage of the sculpting process, Colleen finds her work both fulfilling and healing.

"Watching this person come to life in my hands brings tears to my eyes. Looking at the finished piece and getting startled by the aliveness of the doll tells me that I have indeed captured the likeness and essence of that person."

Because Colleen is in the business of appropriating other people's attitudes, mannerisms, and personalities, she feels it is important for her to always keep an open mind and continue growing and learning in all aspects of her art and her life.

"It's how you evolve as an artist. Focusing on art and artistic pursuits is important, but maintaining a balance between artistic pursuits and the simple pleasures of cooking, gardening, and being with friends is equally important.

"Appreciating other artist's talents and abilities and not enclosing myself in an 'ivory tower' is integral to my work. I learn from others. I try and stay open to life and the things around me so that I stay open to my work and keep delving deeper into my subject matter.

"It's also important to laugh a lot and dance as much as you can!"

Colleen's commitment to experimenting with new methods and materials and improving her technical skills while maintaining a strong connection with her clients are evident in her dolls. She has become adept at working with complicated body poses and balancing vignettes, like Alex and Phil, that include more than one figure and accessory elements.

"I feel like I get to touch my clients' lives. You start off with a little ball of clay and it's hard to imagine the finished product — although I can. I try to feel what they are feeling about what they want in their doll and how to best convey that and then I watch these faces come alive in my hands.

"I love connecting with my clients. I feel blessed and uplifted by it."

To create her "instant heirloom" polymer wedding cake toppers, Colleen requires photographs of the bride's and groom's faces (full face and profile), plus a full-length body shot; photographs of the bridal attire, including the veil, showing drape and detail; and a thorough description of the bouquet. The cake topper can be made for a 6", 7", or 8" base. $1,200.00.

Ashley is a picture-perfect bride. Flawlessly sculpted in porcelain, she stands 18" tall and wears sumptuous silks, satins, and laces in her bridal costume. $1,200.00.

Alex (22") and Phil (24") are polymer clay recreations of two boys and their favorite childhood toys: a G.I. Joe and a dinosaur. "They are wearing sweatshirts and jeans that replicate the outfits they wore as children. They are in their twenties now and I created them at ages three and five. Their mother had expressed a need to show the close relationship between the boys so I worked on poses that would highlight that." $5,000.00 set.

Nikki stands 32" tall and is a polymer clay redhead "full of sass and attitude with her tongue out and hands on her hips." Nikki wears a French blue print dress with lots of petticoats underneath. $6,500.00.

Amy recreates a young woman from New Jersey whose mother commissioned Colleen to cast Amy as a two year old learning to read from a favorite book. The award-winning doll is fully posable and holds an exact copy of the Sesame Street pop-up book shown in the picture from which she worked. In private collection.

Amy: putting the pieces of the puzzle together.

## Jean Lotz

Studio ......................Lacombe, Louisiana
E-mail ......................info@lotzstudiodolls.com
Websites ..................www.lotzstudiodolls.com
                         www.lotzdollpages.com
Medium ..................Wood
Dolls' Price Ranges ..$350.00+
Member ..................The Original Doll Artists Council of
                         America, Inc., the Academy of
                         American Doll Artists, Inc.,
                         the United Federation of Doll Clubs,
                         and the Japanese American Doll
                         Enthusiasts
Museums ................Johnny Gruelle Raggedy Ann & Andy
                         Museum, Arcola, Illinois The Toy &
                         Miniature Museum of Kansas City,
                         Kansas City, Missouri

## Wellspring:

"I stare at people on the street, in newspapers, and in magazines. People completely intrigue me; people of all ages, all sexes, all races — it doesn't matter. Likely it will not be their physical appearance, but their personality, posture, and attitude that capture my attention.

"Later their image will creep into my dreams as a doll. I have vivid dreams about my drawings, paintings, sculptures, and dolls. Sometimes these dreams disturb me until I make an attempt to sketch what I envisioned. I rarely have the time to realize my dreams in paint or traditional sculpture, but I do make an attempt at some of the dolls that jump out of my dreams.

"If I'm very lucky, I'll have my camera with me so I'll ask if I can take a few photos, but generally photos are very disappointing since people freeze up in front of a camera."

## A Hit with Hitty

In the early 1990s, wood carver and doll maker Jean Lotz discovered Hitty, the famous little traveler (she measures just 6¼" tall) from Rachel Field's 1929 Newbery award-winning book, *Hitty Her First Hundred Years*.

So captivated is Jean with this literary lady that she makes what one of her collectors coined as *"Hitty Litters"* — a batch of 10 or so of the tiny wooden wonders at a time, faithfully carving the characters according to the book's illustrations by Dorothy P. Lathrop.

"Although I'm not interested in making the dolls identical, I do get better consistency this way. My collectors like the fact that each Hitty has her own personality: comical, friendly, elegant, stoic."

Jean makes two versions of Hitty. One is made of white ash that is antiqued and distressed and looks like a worn, albeit elegant, three-dimensional version of the doll in the book's illustrations; it is priced at $600.00. The other is carved of American basswood and has painted detailing so that the natural color and grain of the wood shows and sells for $350.00 (nude) and $425.00 (dressed in undergarments). Both types feature the v-shaped butt joint authentic to the original Hitty.

A 6¼" Hitty doll made of white ash ($600.00) and one carved of basswood ($425.00 or $350.00 nude). The doll's name is embroidered in true cross-stitch for the ash doll and in a more simplistic stitch on the chemise of the basswood doll.

‹—◦═◦—›

The original antique folk doll that was bought by Rachel Field at a New York antique store and inspired the book now lives at the Stockbridge Library Association Historical Collections in Massachusetts. The doll has been dated to between the 1830s and 1850s.

"The original Hitty is beautiful, but you can only see this in the three-quarter view of her face; otherwise, she looks stark and badly aged. I wanted my white ash Hitty to look as old as the antique original did, a doll that could have easily endured the ravages of 150-plus years, and who could have undertaken the many adventures mentioned in the book."

## The Healing Power of Dolls

Jean Lotz has a recurring dream wherein she is sculpting gorgeous dolls in porcelain. The visions are always crystal clear and the dolls are invariably fabulous: antique-inspired elegant ladies with an aura of mystery and chock-full of personality. Unfortunately, Jean learned years ago that she is just too clumsy to work in this fragile medium.

"When I worked in porcelain it was a disaster. I broke everything in every stage of creation: prototypes, molds, greenware, and fired pieces! What a mess!"

For now the artist is content to sculpt in wood, to carve her visions in holly, maple, persimmon, bay magnolia, and many other species. A nearly unbreakable medium (unlike porcelain), it is also unforgiving, and Jean must make alterations and compensations to her mental blueprint as she carves. As a result, the doll maker never knows exactly what her finished piece will look like.

"While I will occasionally paint my dolls, I love the look and feel of wood so I don't often hide it. Wood grain is magical to me with its swirling light and dark patterns and it gives each piece its own unique character. It is totally unpredictable. I'm always excited when I drench my carvings into tung oil for the first time. The grain patterns just jump out at that point. I then get my first real glimpse of how this doll might look."

Not the porcelain dolls of her dreams, perhaps, but every bit as fabulous. Jean has been carving dolls since her high school years in the late 1960s, when she would make complex marionettes, dolls, and simple puppets for her own amusement and for gifts for family and friends. Her interest in doll making slowly waned during college, but again piqued in the early 1990s when she created four miniature polymer clay dolls for a competition dollhouse she and a friend built.

"I thoroughly enjoyed making these dolls and was quickly addicted to doll sculpting again."

In the mid-1990s, Jean made a series of 15" girls and boys as an early experiment in using elastic strung ball joints. The artist plans to redesign the joints using springs or mechanical connectors before making anymore in the future. Right now, she is concentrating on her 11" Lotz of Love babies, 1:12 scale dollhouse figures, 1:10 scale dolls, tiny babies intended as doll's dolls, and her beloved Hitty dolls, all carved of wood.

"I also plan to create several much larger figures that would look great in a collection of antique Schoenhut wooden dolls."

In contrast to her more detailed dolls, Jean's tiny "dolls' dolls," whittled from branches of holly, magnolia, and maple, are very stylized creatures that spring directly from her imagination.

"These are not carved to any particular scale. Generally, the size of the tiny bit of wood dictates the size of the eventual doll."

Most of Jean's dolls are based on a set of photographs and detailed drawings. She designs and sculpts each piece from head to toe and designs and makes her own costumes and accessories. She is a pattern-maker, painter, wood carver, seamstress, and embroiderer, filling every role needed to construct her satiny smooth dolls.

She is a prolific picture taker and will photograph a subject extensively if she is interested in capturing a likeness. She is also a collector of antique photos and has an ever-growing stockpile of old family photos.

"I've also been inspired by and enjoy sculpting from out-of-focus photos. I'm interested in capturing a feeling rather than a mirror image of a particular person."

Inspiration is something Jean has learned, through many personal tragedies and trials, to appreciate more fully through her doll making career. It is something the sculptor felt she lost for a time and only regained through the healing nature of doll making.

Suffering what she now believes was a severe reaction to the chemicals in solvents, Jean was unable to deal with everyday tasks in an already complicated life — not to mention carving dolls. Her resulting illness was a slow but increasingly debilitating ordeal characterized by symptoms similar to a mild stroke with severe, blinding headaches.

"Read the back of any petroleum-based solvent container like mineral spirits; I suffered every symptom except for convulsions and death."

Even now Jean remains highly sensitive to solvents, using them with great care if she uses them at all, and she makes it her mission to warn other artists about the hidden dangers in the crafts products they may use. After a long journey to regain her health after her near fatal accidental poisoning due to exposure to these chemicals, Jean is back to work on her dolls, attributing her little wooden wonders with helping her recover.

"The dolls that I made during this period were absolutely horrible but my family loves them. I tried to destroy them on several occasions but my daughter saved them from the fireplace and keeps them as a reminder of how hard I worked to survive this ordeal.

"It's funny but I wouldn't be a professional doll sculptor if I hadn't gotten so very ill. I must credit my doctor for convincing me to quit my high pressure job and to attempt doll sculpting full-time!

"Working on dolls gave me a special creative and physical challenge and provided an important gauge of how I was doing. I could see an improvement in the quality of each new doll. I had visible proof I was healing. You wouldn't believe my pride each time I finished a doll and it smiled back at me!"

Jean put this trial behind her, but soon found herself facing another with the hospitalization and then unexpected death of her mother. Again, she depended on her dolls to help shore up her endurance.

"It's hard to understand how comforting a doll's smile can be until you need one badly! While my mom was in intensive care after open-heart

Lotz of Love Baby, nude to show embroidery work and body construction with wooden button joints, poses with one of Jean Lotz's Hitty Litters. "When seeing all of these Hitty dolls sitting in a basket ready to go, then the term seems very appropriate!" All dolls in private collections.

An 11" Lotz of Love Baby dressed in blue, carved from basswood. Baby has a cloth body embroidered with "Lotz of Love" on the chest and wooden button joints. Jean's Lotz of Love Babies are individually priced, starting at $600.00.

⊰══◯══⊱

surgery, I worked on my dolls. I didn't care how silly I looked as a grown woman sewing a lot of doll clothes in the waiting room. This work kept me very busy so everyone left me alone, but most importantly, it provided stress relief. When I got really horribly unhappy or stressed, I took out my Hitty doll and her smile helped."

Doll making is an important healing tool for both the doll maker and the doll collector. It is Jean's belief that most doll artists are not making dolls for the money but because they need the creative and healing outlets dolls provide.

"Sculpting, designing, sewing, painting, and then getting public exposure and recognition — doll making fills these needs.

"I am always amazed at how many doll artists start making dolls seriously only after some incredible emotional, mental, or physical challenge; so many of them return to a youthful love of dolls to begin a healing process."

Many collectors also enter the world of dolls to "heal themselves from some horrible emotional damage and hurt." Jean believes they need the comfort only can dolls provide.

"It is a very private and personal source of comfort similar to how they felt as a young girl before life took such a toll."

One positive outcome of Jean's recovery was the development of her now massive online research repository of everything relating to the making, collecting, and celebrating of wooden dolls, including what she considers her most personally rewarding doll research in the area of primitive dolls. The "Lotz Doll Pages" initially began because Jean felt like an "oddball" — the only doll maker among her wood carving friends and the only wood carver among her doll making pals.

"I started actively looking for information about any types of wooden dolls from books, magazine articles, auction catalogs, and online auctions. I cover dolls carved from wood, stone, ivory, and other media and categories including antique, modern, ethnic, regional, and character dolls like Hitty. I also include several pages of doll making and carving tips. All is shared freely via the Internet."

⊰══◯══⊱

Jean creates tiny "dolls' dolls" she calls Holly Babies from small holly or magnolia branches that are the size of a given branch Jean split in four pieces. These are the only dolls Jean whittles, carving just for fun and without photo reference material. They have wooden heads and hands on cloth bodies with wire armatures and are dressed in fine cotton batiste and heirloom quality lace. These tiny 5" (or smaller) babies are only available at shows where Jean is making a personal appearance. $100.00.

Maintaining her "Lotz Doll Pages" is time-consuming ("it quickly grew into more than 80 web pages; it's a monster!"), but Jean has her good health back and more time to invest in herself, her dolls, and her research.

"I treasure each moment that I'm working and I feel blessed. I learned a lot of good life lessons from these tests of my endurance, faith, and strength, but I'm healed and back working, eagerly starting to make new original dolls."

And dreaming again of those fabulous porcelain dolls that may eventually become part of the Lotz family of dolls.

Teenage Boy and Teenage Girl are ready for summer fun. Standing 15½" tall and with elastic strung ball joints and hinged knees, both are original, one-of-a-kind dolls carved of basswood that was soaked in tung oil to enhance the grain, the details of which were then painted with artist oils. The contemporary fashions were suggested by Jean's daughter, Allie Lotz. In private collection.

Two Private School Girls, from a mid-1990s original, one-of-a-kind theme group, are carved of solid wood and stand 15½" tall. Carved from basswood and painted with a translucent acrylic glaze, the dolls have elastic strung ball joints and hinged knees. The discontinued dolls were individually priced at $800.00 each.

Closeup of Teenage Girl who wears a carved scrunchy on her carved ponytail. In private collection.

Marcia sculpted the 12" polymer clay Ye Ol' Math Professor in a class taught by master character artist, Annie Wahl, at WOW! 2000 in Concord, New Hampshire. While there, Marcia called her mechanical engineer father, Marvin Dundore, to wish him a happy birthday and tell him that she was working on the doll she planned to give him. His response was, "You're giving me a doll for my birthday?!" Not for sale.

⋆⇢⊶⊶⇠⋆

pinch of chalk in one hand, and a tiny eraser in the other. A pencil pokes out from his wisp of white hair; pens stand ready in his shirt pocket, although without benefit of a pocket protector. The professor's sliver of a tie is askew as are his suspenders.

The artist admits she is constantly making over her dolls to express the originality that is the hallmark of her unique perspective. She has a dozen original doll sculpts in her porcelain doll line, including 32" Samuel, 30" Kimberly, 25" Taylor, and 22" Winnie, who was inspired by the character Winnie Cooper from the 1980s sitcom, *The Wonder Years*. Besides Ye Ol' Math Professor, her one-of-a-kind polymer clay dolls include Storytime, Election Count, and Patty's Parade, among others.

Marcia is also experimenting with a versatile 17" porcelain mold, the first in her "American Woman" series of dolls and one that can be customized. She has made both standing- and bent-leg molds and may design different molds for a variety of arm poses.

"I just wanted to have fun with a doll and be able to do different things with her. I plan to make one-of-a-kind outfits and bridal gowns for her and will be able to customize her hair and eye color."

She has also played with cloth sculpture, in the figure of her Etude for a Violin, using paper clay, muslin, wire, and cotton knit in the three-dimensional cloth tradition of Japanese artist Akiko Anzai.

"This is the most labor-intensive doll I ever made! The doll's face is paper clay and her body is muslin that is stuffed rock hard. A tan knit material is glued and ironed onto it.

"It is a true piece of sculpture."

So far, Marcia has not made additional dolls using this technique, although she has been honing her needle-sculpting skills with a goal of creating more fully realized cloth dolls in the future.

In the meantime, the artist is content to sculpt three-dimensional porcelain and polymer clay portraits

⋆⇢⊶⊶⇠⋆

The patriotic Patty's Parade (16", polymer clay) began with a metal replica of a 1950s bicycle, complete with moving rubber wheels, chain, and pedals, found in a gift shop. Marcia sculpted the doll shortly after September 11 and felt the American flag and red, white, and blue wheel decoration was appropriate. The dog tucked into Patty's basket is made of polymer clay and rabbit fur. "It sheds hairs all over the miniature blanket in the wire basket, just like a real dog." $550.00.

that capture the slice-of-life moments mined from her own background and backyard. She considers each sculpt a learning experience, discovering more about the complexities of human anatomy, as well as about herself and her tastes.

There is 25" Cheerleader Taylor, a porcelain head/Seeley Mod Bod® posable doll which can be customized with school colors — a natural for the former high school teacher.

"Taylor was inspired by a young girl I saw at a wedding reception and was originally costumed in a party dress similar to the one she was wearing at the wedding."

A beloved grandmother rendered in polymer clay and named Storytime Volunteer recalls those wonderful childhood moments of being read to by a well-loved adult from a favorite storybook.

"I cherish those wonderful childhood memories of weeks spent with my grandmother, Erma J. Hurlbert. She had a farm in rural northern Illinois and she had taught in a one-room schoolhouse in the early 1900s. My visits always included a lot of reading."

Marcia's porcelain Reilly and Petey piece was inspired by a redheaded girl she saw in a bowling alley. The little girl came to Marcia's studio and modeled for the doll, holding her finger up as a perch for the tiny 6" parrot that would be sculpted to complete the artist's concept.

"I relived a bit of my past with this doll. I got a blue parakeet I named Petey on my tenth birthday. He was one of my favorite pets."

Petey is a true labor of love for the artist, going through seven firings to build up its layers of color and wing pattern. The end sections of long thin pheasant feathers are then glued into the rump area to create more realistic tail feathers. Reilly's outfit was designed to look very 1950s with rolled-up blue jeans and a blue and white checked, button-down shirt with Peter Pan collar.

"I look back on my childhood days of growing up in the 1950s and '60s with three sisters and two brothers with fond memories. My dolls tend to reflect those days. Coming from a large family, we were not raised with an abundance of frills. This simplicity carries over into my work."

Marcia believes her dolls reflect the honesty and integrity of their creator. More than that, the porcelain and polymer clay figures reflect the wholesome goodness the artist looks for, not only in herself but in her world at large.

"I want people to know that I am a good person and to see that in my dolls.

"My dolls may become more beautiful or they may take on a more whimsical quality, but they will still be mine — made by a small-town, Midwest Christian girl."

The porcelain Reilly and Petey vignette (28" and 6") is the first piece Marcia sold to a famous person — although she didn't realize it until months afterwards — a woman in New Orleans. "I was walking through a bookstore and saw a book turned around with the back cover showing. Feeling the urge to tidy up the shelf, I turned the book around and saw in big letters, "Anne Rice." The inside jacket said that she lived with her husband and son in New Orleans. I grinned to myself all the way out of the store." $625.00

"My younger sister, a program director for the Discovery Center Children's Museum in Rockford, Illinois, needed a Beatrix Potter doll for the traveling Beatrix show that came to the museum one spring. The statuesque, 31" porcelain Bea dressed in her Victorian finery, was the result." (The bunny is made from a reproduction mold since four-legged animals are not the artist's specialty.) $695.00.
Photo by Alan Love

Belle in Her Bonnet (17") is from Marcia's "American Woman" series, available in an unlimited edition for $350.00 each. She has a porcelain head, torso, arms, and legs and can be purchased as a custom-designed bride doll for an additional $50.00 to $100.00.
Photo by Alan Love

The 8" polymer clay Fractured Fairy's Tail is a literal translation of a sculpting challenge, Fractured Fairy's Tale, for which Marcia won the award for Delightfulness of Design at the WOW! 2000 conference. (WOW stands for Week of Workshops and is sponsored by the Academy of American Doll Artists Foundation, Inc.) $500.00.
Photo by Alan Love

# History and Heritage

*"Doll art gets under our skin and into our blood. It speaks vividly to our minds, hearts, and souls."*

*-Monica Reo*

Miss Elizabeth and Mr. Darcy by Monica Reo. Photo by Dick Dettloff. Looking as though they just stepped from the pages of Jane Austin's novel, *Pride and Prejudice*, the porcelain Miss Elizabeth and Mr. Darcy stand 32" and 36" tall, respectively. $8,600.00 set.

# Mary Ellen Frank

Studio ..................... Juneau, Alaska
E-mail ..................... mefrank11@hotmail.com
Website.................... www.niada.org
Media....................... Wood and clay
Dolls' Price Ranges.. $590.00 – $4,000.00
Member.................... National Institute of American
Doll Artists
Museums ................ Seattle Times, Seattle, Washington, permanent corporate collection; Musee de Poupees, Josselin, France, permanent private museum collection; Rosalie Whyel Museum of Doll Art, Bellevue Washington, permanent private museum collection.

## Wellspring:

"The theme or idea that underlies all of my work is the connection of people to the earth. I am interested in indigenous peoples whose integration with nature is clearer, but even in my portrait work of non-native people, I am inspired by the essence that is earthbound, nature-aged. I use wood for most of my work and clothe the dolls in leathers, furs, and natural fabrics, which have generally been worn and broken in."

## It Takes a Village

Alaska doll maker Mary Ellen Frank counts many artists among her circle of dramatic influences. Artist Jane Terzis, an anatomy and portrait drawing professor at the University of Alaska Southeast in Juneau, helped her work on careful observation and capturing a likeness. Terzis earned a Bachelor of Fine Arts degree in painting and drawing from Ohio Wesleyan University as well as a Masters degree in medical and biological illustration, studying physiology and pathology, as well as human anatomy alongside medical students, for her degree.

"Jane is a contemporary and was trained as a medical illustrator and can really see detail."

Dolly Spencer, an Inupiat doll maker from Homer, Alaska, whose work in the Alaska State Museum's travel exhibit and who carves Alaska paper birch dolls with leather bodies, was Mary Ellen's first doll making teacher. Well known in figurative doll circles, Dolly Spencer is a member of the Inupiat tribe who was raised and trained in the old ways and skills. Mary Ellen says that it is Spencer's portrait carvings to which she aspires.

Pioneering doll artist Frances Bringloe, a NIADA doll maker from Seattle, Washington, now deceased, was known for her carved Alaska yellow cedar dolls. Many of her historical dolls are in the permanent collection at the Rosalie Whyel Museum of Doll Art. Bringloe generously shared the details of her carving process which Mary Ellen has largely adopted.

Fred Cogelow, an American master wood carver from Minnesota, remains Mary Ellen's mentor in capturing character with dignity with his incredibly realistic sculpted wood figures.

## *Carving Beautiful People*

For years, Mary Ellen Frank sought work that would feed her soul. A research economist for the State of Alaska by trade, Mary Ellen knew there was an artist trapped within her that needed to be nourished and expressed.

Growing up, Mary Ellen lived on the outskirts of Juneau with artistic, "can-do" parents who filled her life with art and spirit and her hands with creative projects. It was a modus vivendi that became engrained. Even today, Mary Ellen designs and makes most of her own clothes; designs and constructs costumes and sets for theater productions; and registers for at least one art-related course a semester.

Although she made a deliberate decision not to study art in college ("I didn't think I could make a living doing it"), instead pursuing a Bachelor of Arts degree and a Masters degree in economics and political science at McGill University and the University of Michigan, respectively, Mary Ellen continued to follow her artistic impulses. All her free time was filled with classes that would eventually figure intrinsically into her doll making: sewing, ceramics, painting, drawing, fabric surface design, mask making, upholstery, and carving in the tradition of Alaska's northwest coast.

"A course I took that was really fundamental in my turning a corner was on Eskimo doll making, taught by renowned doll maker Dolly Spencer. All the skills and talents I had could be expressed in this art form and here was a woman making a good living doing it.

"I started thinking. . ."

And taking more classes specific to doll making, including a fabric surface design course that was taught by quilt and doll artist Lenore Davis at the Arrowmont School of Arts and Crafts in Gatlinburg, Tennessee, that put her in touch with master doll maker Akira Blount, whose work is in the permanent collection of the Louvre (Musée des Arts Decoratif) and the Musée de Poupees in Josselin, France.

"Akira and I became friends during the course. She invited me to come to her home in Tennessee after I finished taking another fiber arts course that was scheduled for the following week. I visited her for a few days before returning to Alaska, observing her work and work life.

"I kept thinking. . ."

In the fall of 1988, Mary Ellen's life took a tragic and unexpected turn. Her 63-year-old father suffered a heart attack, underwent surgery, and sadly, passed away. Mary Ellen took a leave of absence from her job in Juneau to help her mother, now living south of Seattle, Washington, "adjust and organize her life and space to a new reality."

During the six months Mary Ellen spent with her mother she was amazed to discover the cache of supplies and project ideas her father had dreamed of pursuing "someday."

"As he grew older, my father had less time, energy, and motivation for these projects. It made me see that I needed to make my true interest my job now instead of crowding it into my spare time."

She returned to work for a few months, socking money away and simplifying her life, shedding some possessions (including her house) and storing the rest. After quitting her job, Mary Ellen headed back to Tennessee in late 1989 to apprentice with Akira and learn how to organize her work days, work space, and business. She sold her first two dolls in September of 1990 through a local gallery and, as serendipity would have it, to Helen Hauser, publisher of *Folk Art Magazine.*

"These were small clay-headed dolls in fabric summer parkas (kuspuks) and one had fish skin mukluks and mittens. They were featured in an article on Alaska crafts in the February 1992 issue of the magazine."

Since then, Mary Ellen has continued sculpting dolls in clay and in wood, focusing her work on depictions of northern Native Americans. The doll maker chooses portraits to respectfully show people as they are — or were — at a given moment.

"My work is largely of the elderly, the weathered and worn. These are my 'beautiful people' and they are a group not embarrassed by their age and survival.

"With these subjects, I can explore the objects and clothing that indigenous peoples of northern lands have developed for survival, spiritual connection, tribal pride, and identification."

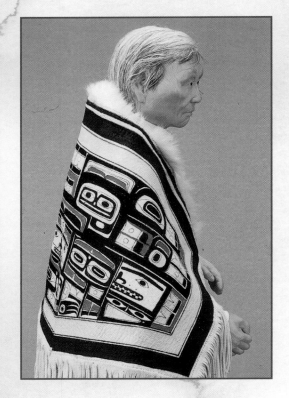

Mack, a Tlingit clan leader, is clad in a contemporary suit, in this case, one made of leathers rather than what in full size would be fabric. He is draped in a Chilkat robe with his clan symbols woven into it. This robe is made of leather, although in full size it is made with cedar bark and mountain goat wool. Mack has Alaska yellow cedar head and arms and hands. $2,685.00. Photo by Jerry Anthony

Mary Ellen's aptly titled Three Generations relationship portrait shows three generations of Eskimo women constructed of Alaska paper birch heads and birch hands.

"The grandmother is teaching her granddaughter to sew by having her construct a small doll. The little girl has an expression of concentration as she sews the ruff on her doll's hood. Mom is bending over to see the progress before heading outside to show off her traditional fancy parka."

In the vignette, the grandmother, Sarah, and the granddaughter, Sheila, wear everyday clothes in contrast to the mother, Irene, who is costumed in dress clothes.

"Grandma's 'housekeeper,' a sewing kit, lies on the floor next to her."

Mary Ellen wants her work to make a very specific statement: that a dignified subject in the hands of a careful, respectful artist can stand on its own.

And stand on its own it does. In Yupik Dancers, a young man named Gary dances and sings unselfconsciously at a community gathering while Frances, an elderly woman, teases and mimics him. Both wear indoor garments with contemporary Eskimo styling. Gary holds male dance fans which are made of bent birch wood and feathers and Frances has female dance fans with coil basketry centers and fur outers. She wears a Yupik woman's beaded necklace (with Siberian trade bead colors) and a headdress with beaded band and fur top.

Pitseolak and Parr features two famous Inuit artists whose work is collected by one of Mary Ellen's own patrons. Clad in traditional Inuit garments, which differ in style and material from Alaskan and Siberian Eskimo wear, the figures' heads are carved of Alaska paper birch. Both stay snug in black muskrat fur clothing.

Mary Ellen's work is informed by traditional doll making techniques. Although she views these as foundation skills and believes they are important to preserve, the artist is willing to abandon tradition for new materials to achieve certain aesthetic purposes.

In Three Generations, Mary Ellen explores relationships between three generations of Eskimo women: grandmother Sarah is teaching her granddaughter Sheila to sew by having her construct a small doll; Sheila concentrates intently as she sews the ruff on her doll's hood; and mom Irene is bending over to see the progress before heading outside to show off her traditional fancy parka. Sarah and Sheila wear everyday inside clothes in contrast to Irene's dress clothes. Grandma's "housekeeper" (sewing kit) lies on the floor next to her. The figures have Alaska paper birch heads; Sarah and Sheila have birch hands. $6,880.00. Photo by Marilyn Holmes

"I have a respect for carving and clothing construction traditions primarily because there is so much knowledge tied up in them. Often I find that there are traditions from another field that apply to the new medium and the means for handling it can be derived from them or mixed with other traditions to get exactly what I want.

"So for me, tradition is where I first look because it likely answers the question I am asking and has been developed by many, over time, who wrestled with the same problems I am struggling with. In cases where tradition does not result in the effect or feel that I want, I have no compunction about mixing and merging traditions or experimenting with new techniques."

Tsimshian Woman Shaman boasts a harmonious blending of traditions with her Alaska yellow cedar head and appendages and cedar bark and ermine headdress. The Northwest Coast Native American shaman is barefooted and holds a globe-shaped rattle. She is wrapped in a squirrel robe protected by a leather apron that is trimmed with clay puffin beaks and cedar rope neck rings and belts.

"I have tried to make my figures as dolls rather than sculptures because I have always liked dolls. It is not really necessary to use this form because they are not really meant for play. It is a confinement or structure that I think still allows for a lot of freedom and adds intrigue.

"It reminds me of the teapots made by artists that are really never meant to serve tea but to honor the form, the situations in which tea is served, and the ceremonies that sometimes surround it.

"In much the same way, I honor the doll form, the subject of human beings, and liveliness of suggested play or playacting."

Pitseolak and Parr are portraits of two famous Inuit artists. Clad in traditional Inuit garments, which differ in style and material from Alaskan and Siberian Eskimo wear, the two figures have heads constructed of Alaska paper birch and fur clothing made of black muskrat. $4,940.00.
Photo by Mary Ellen Frank

In Yupik Dancers Mary Ellen playfully shows young Gary dancing and singing at a community gathering while an elderly woman, Frances, teases and mimics him. Both figures are wearing indoor garments with contemporary Eskimo styling. Gary has male dance fans made of bent birch wood and feathers and Frances has female dance fans with coil basketry centers and fur outers. She wears a Yupik woman's beaded necklace (with Siberian trade bead colors) and a headdress with beaded band and fur top. $5,900.00.
Photo by Marilyn Holmes

Tsimshian Woman Shaman is barefoot and holding an Alaska paper birch globular rattle. She has Alaska yellow cedar head, arms, hands, lower legs, and feet, and wears a cedar bark and ermine headdress, a squirrel robe, leather apron with clay puffin beaks hanging from it, cedar rope neck rings, and belts. $2,950.00. Photo by Marilyn Holmes

Closeup of Tsimshian Woman Shaman. Photo by Marilyn Holmes

# Mary Ellen Lucas

Studio ......................Petersburg, Kentucky
Medium ....................Porcelain
Dolls' Price Ranges ..Dolls are not sold, but given to benevolent groups at the discretion of the artist.

## Wellspring:

"What inspires me is the desire to live each day to the fullest and to help others do the same."

## Doll Dream Team

Mary Ellen Lucas has made over 150 porcelain dolls for her history programs. She has sculpted figures from history, literature, and legend, from the famous folks of the Old Testament to the denizens of the White House. She has made children representing world cultures and plans to create dolls "representing different Scottish clans."

Mary Ellen recently costumed her dream team, the legendary inhabitants of Camelot: King Arthur, the beautiful Guinevere, Lancelot, and Merlin, the wizard and guardian of Arthur.

"I'm not going to do all the Knights of the Round Table, but I'll do some of them, particularly the ones written up from the classic."

Working from illustrations in school books that her mother and later she used in high school literature classes from the 1920s to the 1940s, Mary Ellen is designing ensembles that are elegant and restrained. She plans to hand-embroider some of the symbols shown on the garments that are part of the fabric of the Arthurian legend.

"Arthur was said to be legend for so long and it's a beautiful and fascinating story. He's the legendary figure of the late Middle Ages who has captured the imaginations of most people, but he's also been the subject of historical novels that put him in the sixth century.

"I'm going into more literary things now and Arthur and the rest of these characters will make an interesting program."

## The Doctor of Doll Making

The blue car zipping along the highway looks like many late model Dodge cars on the road these days. What makes it remarkable are its occupants: Joan of Arc, Confucius, Sojourner Truth, Sally Hemming, Socrates, and the Queen of Sheba, along with a half-dozen other Old Testament notables, crowd the back seat.

Queen Esther is one of many Women of the Bible characters. Looking regal in a train of purple velvet with white ermine, Queen Esther may eventually step into the role of Guinevere for Mary Ellen's programs on King Arthur and the Knights of the Round Table.

❖⇒◉⇐❖

Their driver is Dr. Mary Ellen Lucas. At a vivacious 78 years of age, this doctor is still making house (and lecture hall and convention center) calls. Although she limits her travels to regional swings through Kentucky, Ohio, and Indiana these days, Mary Ellen has traveled all over the country with her porcelain entourage, packing up as many as a dozen dolls, depending on the trip's lesson plan.

With 158 "Dolls of Destiny" fired, painted, wigged, costumed, and shelved — and another 16 or so "on the board in various states of undress" — Mary Ellen has taken her design cues from books on history, American literature, and, perhaps her richest source of all: the Bible. She has fired collections of First Ladies, the Children of the World, the Men and Women of History, Our Colonial Background, Native American Indian Culture, and Famous Figures from the Bible.

"I also have a set of Kentucky Heritage Dolls that includes settlers, mountain folk, and a preacher and a collection of Literature of My Childhood dolls. These are all the characters I read about and loved growing up: Little Orphan Annie, the Little Princess, Scarlett O'Hara, Rhett Butler, and others."

The retired high school history teacher, who was awarded her doctorate in education just two weeks shy of her 69th birthday, has been making dolls for nearly 50 years. A chance discovery in her aunt's sewing basket of two antique china heads dating to the Civil War launched a lifelong vocation in molding historic characters. Mary Ellen made Mary Todd Lincoln with one of the china doll heads; the other became Jane Pierce, the wife of fourteenth president Franklin Pierce.

She learned the craft of making porcelain dolls from an award-winning doll maker in northern Kentucky and has worked steadily over the years in her home studio to refine her technique. Mary Ellen is so technically proficient that she was asked several years ago to restore a gift of several antique dolls, including a German Kammer and Reinhardt (K and R) baby doll from the 1870s and a late 1800s china doll, for the Behringer-Crawford Museum in Covington, Kentucky. The dolls are now on permanent display in the museum's nineteenth century history gallery.

At 28", Dancing Elk is a toddler-sized Native American Indian doll of porcelain dressed in elk skin and a beaded headpiece. She has a baby Indian doll in a cradle board. Dancing Elk is included in Mary Ellen's Native American Indian and Children of the World collections.

Mary Ellen's dolls range in size from a petite 11" to an impressive (and weighty) 38" tall. Eyes are either hand-painted or made of glass and manually set in the sculpts. Some molds are bought and some are made by Mary Ellen. All the dolls are the same, according to the doll maker; only the slip — the tinted liquid porcelain — differs.

"For my black dolls I use Seeley's Porcelain Brown Velvet™ Slip. For dolls that represent people from Mexican, Middle Eastern, or Mulatto descent, I mix my own slip with Seeley's Brown Velvet™, French Bisque™ and Indian Flesh™. There's a slip for Oriental dolls and a slip for white dolls that I use for the rest of my dolls.

"Then I add in the paint to achieve the skin tone I want. Every doll I make is fired about five times. It takes this many firings to get the dolls to look right."

All of Mary Ellen's dolls are designed to teach a chapter in history, or a lesson in literature — even a page from sociology or current events. The 28" toddler size Children of the World dolls are used to demonstrate the differences and similarities of world cultures. Her Ira Hayes, an American Indian who fought in World War II (and is featured in the historic Joe Rosenthal photograph of the soldiers raising the American flag atop Mount Surabachi on Iwo Jima), and died of alcoholism, opens discussions on the politics of heroism.

"People say to me, 'I cannot believe you go through all this.' Well, you can only do one thing before you fire it. It's a process. When I made the Children of the World collection, I did 13 dolls in a month and a half.

"I like making the dolls. Why, if I were making a formal, I'd have to get a pattern, size it, cut it, pin it, sew it. There's a certain process you go through in anything you do and doll making is a process, too. There's nothing magic about it. My grandchildren make dolls. They can't do the detail work, but they can blush and clean them beautifully."

Each doll is dressed in period costuming designed by the doll maker: a suit of clothing, necessary millinery, and appropriate accessories including gloves and boots and, in the case of her 11" Winston Churchill, a miniscule cigar clamped in his jaw.

＊→═◎═←＊

Sally Hemming measures 18" tall and is costumed in a French-inspired light lemon yellow dress with a flounce at the bottom. Part of the Black History Group, she was an historical figure that Mary Ellen had read about for years. "I thought it was time we recognized Sally Hemming as a Lady of the White House."

Measuring a diminutive 11", Winston Churchill is in the Men of History collection. "He told it like it was, warts and all, and he got kicked out of every school he ever went to. He didn't fit the conventional pattern. But in World War II, he would give you hope. He gave me hope. Historic figures have done that through the years."

A faithful follower of the reuse-reduce-recycle school of thought, Mary Ellen assembles most of her ensembles from secondhand store discards. The organza gown with flounced and ruffled shirt for her 36" Marie Antoinette was designed from two thrift shop formals that cost just $2.00. The gold lamé coat sported proudly by her 36" Henry VIII is edged with a real mink collar stitched up from a cast-off fur coat. Many of Mary Ellen's Native American Indian dolls, a favorite subject of the doll maker, are outfitted in real leather made from purses bought at Goodwill stores and cut down for tunics, breeches, and footwear.

Breastplates and other adornments are culled from the buckles and beads of purse trims and have been integrated into the wardrobes of Crazy Horse, Sequoia, Sitting Bull, Tecumseh, Hiawatha, and Jim Thorpe. Biblical characters — everyone from Eve to Queen Esther, even Jezebel — have fared equally well in the fashion department. A shield crafted from a large button, made in the 1800s and featuring a Roman bust set in bas-relief, became an accessory for a prophetess found in the Book of Judges.

"It came off the coat worn by the mother of a friend who found it in an old trunk. That button must be 2" across. It made a wonderful shield and I used it for Deborah who's in my Women of the Old Testament collection."

Depending on the program, these dolls and others travel in all their recycled finery with Mary Ellen on teaching trips, recounting their history to business, church, social, alumni and missionary groups and clubs. Alice in Wonderland and her coterie, Dancing Elk, the three Wise Men, and Secondhand Rose (a homeless woman), have all been guests of honor at one of Mary Ellen's excursions into history.

"Dolls articulate history by presenting a visual representation of historic figures. They emphasize the human qualities of historic persons."

Recently, at the request of a young member of the Daughters of the American Revolution, she made a doll of Mary Desha, a native of Lexington, Kentucky, who co-founded the organization in 1890. The group wanted to make a complete wardrobe and trunk for the doll to raffle off for the DAR. Mary Ellen located clothing patterns from the 1890s and delivered them, along with the doll, to the chapter in Lexington, Kentucky.

"By using dolls in historic programs, it lets others experience the past that is so necessary in understanding today and in hoping for great things in the future."

Confucius stands 18" tall and is included in the Men of History collection, men whom Mary Ellen believes changed philosophical thought. "Certainly Confucius did that."

Alice in Wonderland, the Queen of Hearts, Mad Hatter, and the Rabbit are in the Literature of My Childhood collection. From the time Mary Ellen was little, her moments alone had to do with reading and when she read *Alice's Adventures in Wonderland*, she felt that she didn't just share Lewis Carroll's story but, "in my mind I was sharing all these other stories, of slipping through this big hole and having all sorts of adventures." Mary Ellen believes Carroll shared age-old stories that enthrall one generation after another and help children understand the difference between fantasy and reality.

## Monica Reo

Studio ....................Eastpointe, Michigan
E-mail .....................Monicareo@aol.com
Website ..................http://www.creationsinporcelain.com
Medium...................Porcelain
Dolls' Price Ranges ..$4,000.00+
Member..................Artists United

## Wellspring:

"Inspiration begins with a visual concept. It may be something I see in a movie, a book, or even a particularly beautiful fabric that immediately sets my mind to work. I sometimes use period fashion books and some paper doll books to inspire my imagination and build on from there.

"My ideas mostly begin in my mind's eye and snowball from there! I start visualizing the actual doll: her coloring, her eyes, her hair, and of course, her gown and shoes. I can spend days with my fabrics, books, and sketches. I will sometimes even wake from a sound sleep if inspiration penetrates from my subconscious musings.

"When an idea comes to me, I must put it on paper immediately. I must say, I do love this process! To be able to bring to fruition what you see in your mind is so incredible and freeing."

## Preserving History

"Dolls preserve a sense of history by showing us the costumes of particular eras and countries. An historically accurately dressed doll makes history come alive both to adults and children in a way that no simple illustration on a page can achieve. It helps us understand that real people wore these different fashions during earlier times and/or in different countries. However, it could be said that we learn these things and not realize we are learning because we are having fun looking at a beautiful doll."
-Fay Zerbolio, board member of the Miniature Museum of Greater St. Louis.

## An Enchanted Collector

"Our home is often called 'The Enchanted House' by friends and visitors with whom we share our art collections and our love of art, fine craftsmanship, and beautiful things! Our collections of pottery, sculptural glass, paintings, and fiber are interwoven throughout our home, but what makes our home charming, warm, inviting, and welcoming are the artist dolls designed by Monica Reo.

"They are interspersed throughout our home: expectantly greeting our guests at the top of the stairs; dancing in the living room; initiating conversation! Our collection includes a ballerina on her toes, a New Orleans Creole belle, a Venetian beauty dressed for a masked ball, a Parisian peasant, and a striking Courtesan.

"Although we own large-sized artist dolls by Pat Thompson and Jan McLean, Monica's are executed with unparalleled detail, from fingernails and leather shoes to exquisitely designed clothing (undergarments and all), along with exceptional fabric choices and gifted stitchery. The hand-painted eyes fascinate our guests, who look closely — and still cannot believe they are painted!

"What we also like are the color choices of the faces and overall body expressions of these young ladies that can be posed and manipulated so their gestures are life-like — a snapshot taken at a selected moment in time.

"'A thing of beauty is a joy forever,' said Keats. For those who have never had the pleasure of meeting Monica, she is as lovely and gracious as her dolls. As dedicated collectors of art, we believe Monica Reo is one of the best kept secrets in contemporary doll making."

-Sherry Schmidli
Clinton Township, Michigan

## *A Passion for Fashion*

Monica Reo loves to bring the history of the Renaissance, Victorian, Edwardian, and Napoleonic eras alive — at least the light-hearted, romantic side of history — through her exquisitely feminine and flawlessly sculpted porcelain dolls.

"History is as glorious as it is terrible and sad. Beautiful fashions were often created and worn under hardships and adverse conditions.

"To me, history comes alive in the dolls I make in that I am able to create my ideas with a twist of pure frivolity and without the grimness and harshness of reality."

Monica's 38" Juliette personifies Monica's passion for the classical beauty of the Renaissance and her penchant for suitably elaborate costumes. She is fitted in sumptuous style in a gold-flecked burgundy silk knit edged flirtatiously with rhinestone-studded tapestry and low-slung bejeweled belt. With a burnished crown of curls and tapestry slippers peeking out from her modestly slit gown, Juliette is all prim poise and fashion-plate femme — the very embodiment of royalty.

With her sculpts, the award-winning artist feels her greatest challenge lies in expressing a paradigm of dreamy innocence and worldly sophistication. Her goal is to create a realistic image capable of evoking heart-felt emotion, one whose individual personality is perfectly suited to its temporality along history's timeline.

Juliette personifies Monica's passion for the Renaissance period with a twist of imagination. She wears a gown of elaborate gold-flecked silk knit, trimmed with a rhinestone tapestry and jewelry to finish the look. The 38" Juliette has a haughty countenance, a true presence of royalty. $4,800.00.
Photo by John Reo

Simone is every inch the well-bred courtier from eighteenth century France in her periwinkle violet silk and velvet frock accented by black netting and burnout velvet patterned appliqués. Giavanna, a lady of the Italian courts, is a vision of old-world fashion in layers of silk, taffeta, and brocade in pale and dusty rose accessorized with leather burgundy pumps.

"Sculpting is an evolving experience and process for me. I strive for the perfect combination of the doll's expression, character and pose with a complimentary color palette and costume design. I hope to establish an 'identity of design' where my dolls are different yet have distinct similarities that identify my personal signature."

Monica grew up with an appreciation for and a love of dolls. As cherished childhood Christmas gifts from her parents, Monica treasured her dolls and still has fond memories of her favorite: a Madame Alexander Alice in Wonderland. Dolls also figured prominently in bedtime fairytales read to young Monica by her mother.

"These wonderful stories would take my imagination to a magical place of knights in armor, glorious castles and, of course, a beautifully and meticulously dressed princess."

A former cosmetologist and advanced hair and color technician, Monica has been sculpting original dolls since 1992 when her husband, John, insisted she try working in porcelain — "despite its unforgiving nature." She had spent the previous ten years making reproduction dolls, deriving most of her pleasure from the painting and costuming phases. She already knew how to sculpt, having attended the College for Creative Studies at Wayne State University in Detroit as well as seminars in the field of fine doll art presented by renowned classical sculptor Janice Trimpe and master European artist Philippe Faraut.

Thanks to John, Monica decided to put her passions and skills to work in original, one-of-a-kind fine art dolls, the ladies' fair that began taking shape in the future artist's childhood imaginings. It is a decision that has paid off for the doll maker on several levels: personal fulfillment, recognition in the doll world, and accolades from collectors. Fans all over the United States and in Europe covet such beguiling damsels as the comely Gabrielle, a doll that took shape after Monica watched the 1998 movie, *Ever After*, a modern retelling of the Cinderella fairy tale.

"Gabrielle has a kind of reality Cinderella theme. Her dress is beaded and appliquéd trim overlaid on pale blue twinkle organza with a cream pearl embroidered organdy skirt and train. She even has silver beaded and sequined mules like Danielle wore in the movie."

Monica's earlier cosmetology training is evident in the carefully made up hair and faces of her dolls,

Gabrielle's dress is beaded and appliquéd trim overlaid on pale blue twinkle organza with a cream pearl embroidered organdy skirt and train. "I created Gabrielle after I watched the movie, *Ever After*. It had a reality Cinderella theme." She stands a full 34", from her gem-studded tiara to her beaded and sequined mules. $4,800.00. Photo by John Reo

The stately 36" tall La Contessa Giavanna is a tribute to Monica's own Italian and French roots. "Giavanna has a very regal presence. She is the rich and beautiful wife of a very prominent and successful European merchant and vintner from the 1800s." The doll's burgundy and rose silk brocade day gown reflects the wealth and comfort of her life. $4,800.00.
Photo by John Reo

from finely arched brows to shadowed and lined eyes to contoured and blushing cheeks. Wigs are typically made of human hair or mohair and in warm color palettes (honey red, mahogany red, golden honey blonde, burnished auburn), the voluminous tresses chicly dressed with feather or gemstone tiaras, silk bows or bonnets, or frothy veils of bridal tulle. Each doll's hands are curved delicately and each slender finger is glossed with liquid acrylic or coated with a porcelain nail.

Creating just ten to 12 delicate pieces each year, Monica devotes herself to her dolls, firing each one as many as ten times to achieve a vibrant translucence. Using a china painting technique she developed with the encouragement of sculptor Ron Booker, Monica hand-paints the eyes in luminous shades of emerald, amber, and teal.

One of the doll maker's favorite subjects quickly became the fashions of England's Victorian era, the late 1800s to early 1900s, although most of Monica's designs bear the imprint of her own European heritage, particularly her Italian and French ancestry. Her dolls' faces also reflect this influence with beautifully exotic visages, gracefully slender necks, and coquettish décolleté.

"My heritage is seen in my sculpting and my costuming. The periods of fashion from the French and Italian Renaissance to the era of Louis XIV and down to the French Revolution and French Restoration inspire me greatly. There is much freedom in movement and less rigorous details in the designs from these eras. When I sketch my concepts and drape fabrics of silk, lace, and beaded trims into a gown design, I can let my fantasies in costuming come to life."

La Contessa Giavanna, a tribute to Monica's Italian and French roots, is fantasy personified in all its curvaceously full-figured glory. The rich and beautiful wife of a prominent European merchant and vintner of the 1800s, Giavanna is a statuesque 36" and exudes regal presence with her burgundy and rose silk brocade day gown that reflects the wealth and comfort of her life.

Much of Monica's time is spent researching costume styles so that she can accurately depict the designs and trends of the historic era represented by a doll's ensemble. The value of her research is evident in pieces like the 34" Madelaine, a bride from the turn of the last century. Monica studied bridal fashions from 1899 to 1905 to create the doll's diaphanous, layered confection of silk chiffon and soft white, beaded and sequined silk overlay skirt and bodice.

"Each historic period has very distinctive features and concepts in its fashion designs. Capturing these principles gives the costuming authenticity.

"Today's women have absolute freedom in their dress code; style and garment restrictions are virtually non-existent. While I do love this freedom, I appreciate the gentle romantic and feminine shapes of historic costumes."

Jacquelyn is a commission for a collector in Switzerland. The collector wanted the 38" piece to be costumed in a gown of mauve and rose silk from the Napoleonic era. $4,800.00. Photo by Dick Dettloff

Jacquelyn, a commission for a collector in Switzerland, comes from the pages of Napoleonic history. Standing 38" tall and wearing a gown of mauve and rose silk with full skirt and fitted bodice that is accented by a jeweled lavaliere, Jacquelyn resembles a member of France's mid-1800s aristocracy.

Miss Elizabeth and Mr. Darcy, 32" and 36" tall, respectively, look as though they just stepped from the genteel English parlor of Jane Austen's 1813 novel, *Pride and Prejudice*. Miss Elizabeth is resplendent in Monica's nod to the Romantic era: a lavender floral gown with fitted jacket and matching reticule and bonnet sashed with periwinkle ribbon. Mr. Darcy cuts an elegant figure in his olive green tails over even darker olive green jodhpurs and chocolate brown leather riding boots.

Alissa is the doll maker's concept of Snow White. The 34" doll is swaddled in silver-lined burgundy hood and silver toile pashmina over a burgundy sequined silk gown with pewter metallic organdy trim. The richness of the gown stands in sharp but complimentary contrast to Alissa's pale complexion, blue-gray eyes, and raven hair.

"I think the most rewarding aspect in doll art and the related research is having the freedom to incorporate the beauty of these intricate and elaborate fashions with my own imagination.

"Throughout history, changing fashions were in essence the foreplay of courting rituals. It was fashion (then and now) that drew the attention to the opposite sex through one's appearance and attire."

Closeup of Alissa, a fairytale-gorgeous depiction of Snow White in her rich burgundy sequined silk gown with pewter metallic organdy trim. Measuring 34" tall, Alissa has a flawless complexion and a glossy crown of raven hair. $4,800.00.
Photo by Dick Dettloff

Madelaine is the artist's vision of a bride wearing the kind of gown she would have loved to wear if she had lived at the turn of the last century. Monica researched bridal fashions from 1899 to 1905 to create her multi-layered design of ivory silk chiffon with soft white beaded and sequined silk overlay skirt and bodice. Madelaine is 34" tall. $4,800.00.
Photo by John Reo

Closeup of Madelaine.
Photo by John Reo

# Otherworld

*"People always tell me that my fairies look like they are hiding a secret or know something special. When I accomplish that then I know that I've instilled a bit of my own soul into that piece of art and it makes me happy."*

-Karen Morley

The Fairy's Boudoir by Karen Morley. This come-hither fairy is made of polymer clay, as are her sturdy, albeit dainty-looking wings. She is ornamented with delicate netting and semi-precious stones and her sleep chamber is adorned with velvet leaves and flowers and beaded garlands and festoons. The vignette measures nearly 10" tall. $125.00.
Photo by Karen Morley

## Karen Morley

Studio .......................Eau Claire, Wisconsin
E-mail .......................vinylgirl@charter.net
Website ...................www.littledoll.com/petite_fantasy/
                              (Doll Repaints & Sculptures)
                              www.littledoll.com
                              (Vintage Barbie®)
Media .......................Polymer clay, mixed media
Dolls' Price Ranges..$400.00 – $3,000.00
Member ...................United Federation of Doll Clubs, Inc.

## Wellspring:

"Emotion! My emotions are the force behind my work. What I create depends upon my emotions at the time. Of course, my family is the most important thing in my life and my emotions toward my family really affect my work. (Oddly enough, though, other people that I meet sometimes seem to affect it more.)

"I'm very influenced by the people in my life, especially my father and my grandfather. My father is my ideal of a good and fun person and I have looked up to him all my life. I once created a piece called Grandpa Geezer, a sweet, old ogre that reminded me of my father.

"Often when I create a piece I do not know that I am creating someone I know or love until my work is finished. Then someone will come along and look at my piece and say, 'That looks just like your dad or your mother,' or someone else in my family. That's the magic part of making dolls."

## Online Doll Art Show

The first online wholesale doll trade show, the brainchild of Karen Morley who combined creative forces with four other original doll artists, opened for business in January, 2003. The private shows are targeted to gallery and shop owners and web-based retailers of dolls and doll art.

Karen's goal was to give artists the opportunity to show their work to retailers through a central site on the Internet that is accessible and easily navigable. The group of artists now includes seven doll makers who have distinguished themselves through beautiful and innovative creations. They include Kim Jelley, Gail Lackey, Marilyn Radzat, and Karen Williams Smith, each an original, one-of-a-kind artist whose style is as unique and individual as a fingerprint.

Potential buyers register (for free) to attend the shows and must be genuine storefront or website retailers/stockists. Interested collectors must contact the various retailers to make their purchases.

When show time comes, Karen adds the database for the retailers and then no one else can get into the show because it is closed off to everyone who is not in that database. The next day, Morley removes the database after all of the retailers have made their purchases on the first day of the show. With that database removed, anyone can then get into the show.

Visit the Doll Art Show at www.doll-art-show.com.

Looking like she's hiding the world's biggest secret is tiny "Vineyard Faerie," a 6" polymer clay fantasy figure dressed in floral crown and trimmed with vibrant wings, velvet leaves, and sparkling baubles. $700.00.

—✦═══○═══✦—

has a deep-dimpled smile and come-play-with-me eyes.

Wearing torn chiffon and vintage velvet leaf and petal adornments along with durable, posable wings, Vineyard Faerie is at once delicate and sturdy and ready for a romp among the flowers. Her ready smile hints that there will be plenty of time to stop and smell the roses.

"As an artist, I pray that my fairies and other creatures will influence the lives of the people who buy them in a good and happy way."

"I hope that when collectors look at my work they get a very good feeling from it."

Articulating her love of family, expressing her emotions and evoking mood through color and color combinations are all of equal importance to Karen.

"This is the spring I dip into for my creativity. Family and emotion affect my moods. The feelings that I experience each day affect the colors that I choose. All are intertwined to inspire me to create."

Karen has been so successful at investing her emotions in her fairies that collectors have told her that the little figures look like they are hiding a secret or know something special that they will tell only when they are ready.

In this way, the dolls are the spitting image of their creator.

"Everyone tells me that I look like I know something that I'm not telling. When I sculpt children, they look the same way. My children are always otherworldly — usually of the fairy realm.

"It's where I'd really love to be in life if I could — in that realm of fantasy and magic."

—✦═══○═══✦—

Flame is a Brenda Starr repaint, stunningly beautiful in her flawless make-up and perfectly coiffed auburn tresses. With a ruby lavaliere about her neck, matching gemstones on her ears, and just the wisp of black netting above her brow, Flame is every ounce the coquette. $350.00.

The beguiling Sapphire is a fiery femme wearing body art and beautiful paper wings sparkling in the color of her name. The 7" polymer clay fairy perches on an antique velvet box. $275.00.
Photo by Karen Morley

One of Karen's fashion doll fantasy make-overs, Duireena is a strong and sensual warrior fairy adorned in shimmering wings and vintage fabric and trims. $275.00.
Photo by Karen Morley

## Anna D. Puchalski

Studio ......................New York, New York
E-mail ......................angeldevildolls@aol.com
Website ..................http://members.aol.com/angelspoon
Media ......................Polymer clay, resin
Dolls' Price Ranges..$50.00 – $1,000.00
Member..................Academy of American Doll Artists, Inc.

## *Wellspring:*

"I need to keep myself motivated so I read books, watch movies, and listen to music to get in the mood to sculpt or to get my ideas stirring, but that primary base is just somewhere deep in my brain and always has been. It just needs to be woken up a bit. My best ideas are always the internal ones."

## *In Search of "Otherworld"*

For Anna Puchalski, "otherworld" is a place in the mind — anything from Lewis Caroll's Wonderland to H.P. Lovecraft's Kadath, or even Eveylyn Waugh's Hollywood in *The Loved One*. It is a vision of the artist's creation.

Some of the artist's favorite "Otherworlds" in print:

The comically grotesque, child-empowering worlds created by Roald Dahl, author of *James and the Giant Peach, Charlie and the Chocolate Factory, The Witches* and *Matilda*, among many other books and screenplays.

Edward Gorey's somewhat sinister worlds in *The Gashlycrumb Tinies, The Doubtful Guest,* and *The Wuggly Ump*, as well as over 100 other works, plus appropriately offbeat and ominous set and costume designs for innumerable theater productions and a prodigious body of pen and ink illustrations in publications such as *The New Yorker* and *The New York Times* and in books by Charles Dickens, John Updike, Virginia Woolf and H.G. Wells, among others.

The epic worlds of Lewis Carroll, famous creator of *Alice's Adventures in Wonderland, Through the Looking-Glass, The Hunting of the Snark,* and *Sylvie and Bruno.*

The "Never Lands" of JM Barrie, author of Peter Pan, and whose prolific body of plays includes *Quality Street, The Admirable Crichton, Dear Brutus,* and *Mary Rose.*

H.P. Lovecraft's macabre worlds in such tales as *The Alchemist, The Tomb, The Thing on the Doorstep,* and *The Horror in the Burying-Ground.*

On the silver screen:

*City Of Lost Children*, 1995, French with English subtitles. A fairy tale for adults, with all the dark and scary undertones expected from traditional fairy tales.

*Evil Dead 2: Dead by Dawn*, 1987. A stylized send-up of the horror genre that is a cult favorite with its spectacular special effects and complete with teenagers, zombies, decapitations, and the requisite ramshackle far-from-nowhere cottage that appears deserted — but not for long.

*Phantom of the Paradise*, 1974. A Brian De Palma tour de force with horror nimbly mixed with music and comedy.

*The Red Shoes*, 1948. Classic dark fairy tale about the power, beauty, and magic of passion and its ability to destroy.

*Singing in the Rain*, 1952. A silent world, a talking world, a dream sequence, a presence hidden behind the curtain, a musical montage of "otherworlds" starring everyone's favorite song and dance man, Gene Kelly.

## An Enchanted Tableau Vivant

With the announcement that a vinyl doll would be made from one of her designs, New York doll artist Anna Puchalski experienced a defining moment in her doll making.

"My first reaction was, 'Oh, this is incredible!' followed by, 'Will anyone really want to buy a vinyl doll I designed?' followed by, 'Who cares, this is so cool!'"

Anna was exhilarated.

The self-described split personality and, at age 28, one of the youngest working artists on the contemporary original art doll scene, Anna and her Angel Devil creations seem poised for international celebrity. Her 11" fully posable Waif, a vinyl doll limited to 666 pieces of each design, will be sold in Hong Kong, China, and Japan through Toy2R, which also distributes her limited and special edition Qee® Series doll keychains featuring skewed interpretations of a white and silver Angel Bear and a black Evil Cat, throughout Asia, Europe, and the United States.

"Raymond Choy, the man behind Toy2R, seems to have a lot of faith in me and my designs. Designing Waif was an incredible experience and one that required me to return to comics because the doll will have her own comic strip."

Selling her Waif design is just the latest feather in the cap of one of the industry's most prolific doll makers.

With an eye for the grotesqueries of the netherworld combined with the beauty of animation, Anna has created a cast of strikingly arresting characters that includes wraiths, vampires, demons and devils, fairies, crackle dolls, and angels in red gym shoes.

She has made literally hundreds of dolls in her nearly ten years in the business and all reflect the latest innovations of contemporary technology melded seamlessly with the values of old-world construction. From a 5" Mexican devil figurine that caught on and sold out almost immediately to her Undead Bunnies that have collectors "rabbit-crazy" for more, Anna's work is selling all over the world. That puts a grin on her face that rivals that of Lewis Carroll's Cheshire Cat's — a character that happens to be one of her favorite (and bestselling) dolls, even though she has an admittedly "darker" view of *Alice's Adventures in Wonderland* than most readers.

"Alice is in a magical world, but she's not having a

The Qee® series doll keychains feature otherworldly interpretations of a white and silver Angel Bear and a black Evil Cat. They are part of the Toy2R Series 3 Designer Collector special edition. $50.00 HK (about $7.00 U.S.). Illustration courtesy of Toy2R.

Anna designed one of her Alice in Wonderland sets with a specific purpose in mind: "I wanted to do a deluxe set with the Queen of Hearts and I imagined her as being part upholstered chair." The fully jointed, polymer clay set includes 5" Alice, a 5½" Queen of Hearts with four cards, and a 4" White Rabbit, each dressed in silk. The Queen has wire legs. Anna also included accessory items (crown, watch, and flamingo) that she also sculpted. $275.00.

very good time. Sometimes it's down right frightening for her; other times she's simply irritated.

"I like these aspects of the story and my Alice dolls tend to reflect that. The story seems less a happy childhood tale to me and more a dark dream."

Like so many of Anna's dolls, her Alice figure is a throwback to the doll maker's childhood that blended her admiration of morbid minimalist Edward Gorey, an illustrator, author, and playwright she grew up wanting to emulate, and style and fashion trailblazer Sasha Morgenthaler, a Swiss doll designer.

Anna's own dolls tend to celebrate this dichotomy, encompassing a mixed bag of one-of-a-kind, direct-sculpt polymer clay pieces, limited edition dolls, and vinyl figures based on the artist's designs and featuring jointed limbs using a variety of techniques that allow maximum movement. All of Anna's dolls are interactive art constructed for adult play and not intended for young children.

To give her dolls the illusion of movement and emotion, Anna employs an old European puppetry trick she calls Black Eye and now considers to be her personal calling card in doll design. Favored by Swiss, German, and Czechoslovakian puppet makers, the technique requires setting the hand-painted black eyes of her dolls with cubic zirconium jewels. The stones catch the light and animate the dolls' faces.

"Some people find this a little scary, but I like it because it brings out the dolls' inner personalities."

Although not all of Anna's dolls have jewel-set eyes, most of them do have painted eyes, the technique favored by the former illustrator and her most dedicated fans. A few of Anna's dolls, including her Glass-Eyed Fairy and limited editions, have glass eyes.

"Sometimes glass eyes can give a doll's face a dolly look, meaning they stop having the appearance of art and look like a traditional doll, but usually the effect is rather pleasing."

Anna's 12" polymer clay Glass-Eyed Fairy has cellophane wings and a leather dress that evokes images of woodland larks and lighting on favorite flowers. This doll came into being after Anna decided to play with mismatched eyes and loved the effect. $200.00.

Undead Bunny Rabbits are made of polymer clay and painted with acrylics. They are jointed, sport blackened eyes, and pack a lot of attitude. $50.00 – $55.00.

Because of the eye settings, joints, and themes that explore and revel in incongruous distortions of the traditional, Anna's dolls are frequently referred to as puppets. Her doe-eyed vampire dolls in their diaphanous red gowns are darkly fascinating. Her wraiths are more substance than shadow and cast an eerie aura with their jewel-set eyes. Even Anna's angels strike an inharmonious note, sporting red sneakers because the shoes give them an "earth-bound" quality.

"I tend to make specific characters that have a purpose. They are beautiful things you can interact with."

All of Anna's dolls are jointed from head to toe, each boasting a complex ball joint system the artist developed herself. Even her tiniest figurines (some measure just 3" and 4" tall) move at the necks, arms, elbows, torsos, hips, knees, and ankles. Because of the painstaking thought and effort, as well as the endless hours of research, development, and refinement that Anna invested in this sculpting technique, she considers it to be a trade secret.

Her recently designed 12½", 50-piece limited edition Cocoa is a strikingly beautiful doll sculpted of Flumo slip and constructed with 13 points of articulation in a variation of her signature ball joint system. Cocoa's face radiates energy and emotional presence compliments not only of Anna's "Black Eye" technique, but also of glass inset and hand-painted applications. She is outfitted with removable clothes to encourage her buyers to interact freely with her.

Inspired by Richard Adams's bunny-centric epic, *Watership Down*, Anna created a warren of figures called Undead Bunnies which will join her other creations at Toy2R.

"A collector of mine ordered about 13 Undead Bunnies over the course of a few months. She showed them to her friend, who happened to be Raymond Choy of Toy2R. He decided I had an Asian aesthetic and the next thing I knew I was working on designs for his Qee® series and my own Waif doll, as well as the Undead Bunnies.

Based on what the artist calls her odd view of the leapus family, Anna's rabbits are classified as both lovely and cute, as well as gross and sometimes very ugly.

"I find them to be very human. My prevailing memory of rabbits is that they die very easily. I think my childhood pet rabbits were my first introduction to death. So I wondered, 'What happens to all those cute, fuzzy, dead bunnies?' Maybe they become zombies!"

Anna's Crackle dolls are the embodiment of her imaginings of what old wood or paper pulp dolls that have lain too long in the attic would look like. Sculpted from polymer clay and painted and given a distressed finish, the dolls sport sculpted corsets, layers and layers of varnish, and lost and abandoned expressions.

Anna's vinyl 11" posable Waif features an injection-molded body with jointed knees, shoulders, and hips, and a vinyl rotocast head. Many designs will be available, each limited to 666 pieces, with the first edition named Waif in Wonderland. Waif is a ⅙ scale doll based on Anna's design and comes with a Qee figure and accessories.
Illustration courtesy of Toy2R.

"The Crackle dolls just came about one night. I wanted to make a doll that looked antique without being a reproduction of the penny dolls that were sold in general stores in the 1800s."

Most Crackles are designed as ballerinas, Victorian ladies or children, and, lately, circus performers. The Crackle ballerinas, called Pavlovas for the renowned Russian ballerina, come in different sizes, the largest of which are sold in hand-painted Pavlova's boxes.

Many of Anna's creations, like the Crackle dolls, Tiny Fairy, assorted vampires, imps, and mermaids are the result of the artist's flights of fancy. Some emerge from experiments. Her Glass-Eyed Fairy was built piecemeal from samples of doll making products Anna received in the mail.

"I wanted to see if I could do a one-of-a-kind with glass eyes. The piece started with a head and mismatched eyes. I liked the head so much I made a body and she became a fairy."

She says her Girl Witches and Girl Ghosts are just pure fun to make. The 7" tall, fully jointed figures show Anna's penchant for creating otherworldly beings that so many collectors find simply enchanting.

"In some ways, all of these creatures and characters are just residents of the fictional place my imagination lives in — where being a witch, vampire, or ghost is not a bad thing, where cute little critters often have lots of teeth, and where Tinkerbell is more of an insect than a person."

⊷⸗⊜⸗⊶

At 6", Anna's polymer clay Crackle dolls, including her themed Antique Circus Performer with silk ribbon skirt are dollhouse-size perfect. Achieving the look of old wood or paper pulp dolls, long forgotten in their attic storage, requires layer upon layer of varnish. They are given distressed finishes and sold dressed or stripped down to their underpinnings. $100.00.

# Marilyn Radzat

Studio ....................Kahuku, Hawaii
E-mail ....................ikons@hawaii.rr.com
Website ..................www.marilynradzat.com
Media ....................Polymer and resin clays, mosaic
                         tile, antique fabric and trim,
                         found objects
Dolls' Price Ranges..$2,000.00 – $6,000.00
Member..................National Institute of American
                         Doll Artists
Museums ................The Puppenmuseum in Spain
                         and Germany

## Wellspring:

"In the beginning, my inspiration came from antique pieces of fabric that conjured up images of ladies in gowns. Upon moving to Hawaii, it was the magical sea glass, scattered on the sand like jewels, that filled me with inspiration, and this led me to using more hardscapes and mosaics to create costumes, form, and style.

"More recently, I find that I am able to put myself, by choice, into a mindset where I am in Otherworld and images fill my internal vision. I no longer need a physical item to take me there, but can go by choice. It has become a practiced state of mind, a meditation, and the place where I am the most at home."

## The Legend of the Maryhoonies™

On a small island in the middle of the Pacific Ocean lives a unique and curious clan: The Maryhoonies™. Named for the ancient Menehune tribe (a magical people who dwell in the Hawaiian Islands) and the modern Mary Jane black patent leather shoes worn by generations of little girls, they are themselves enchanted.

The chubby-cheeked "Hoonies," as Marilyn Radzat calls her one-of-a-kind polymer clay shell creatures, range in size from 2" to 12" tall and in price from $130.00 to $500.00. Each is fitted with a shell that washes up from the ocean and trimmed with found objects. Their luminescent personalities glow in their sweet-natured faces and are reflected in the shine of their slick little shoes.

The Maryhoonies™ inhabit a realm "just beyond. . . just around the corner. . . just beyond our eyesight.

A family of Maryhoonies™ show off the fun, flair, and fantasy Marilyn brings to these tiny shell creatures steeped in legend and lore. All but the tiniest wear the shiny black patent leather shoes that inspired their name. $130.00 – $500.00.

Friends depicts a little creature with wings and mosaic cap reaching toward a tiny Maryhoonie™ sea creature, a signature Radzat design. $2,000.00.
Photo by Linda Ching

Contemplation sits cross-legged on a little pedestal doing just what her name implies. Made of polymer clay, she shimmers in variegated shades of bronze and is costumed in beautiful web-like antique metallic lace. She wears a real leaf, dipped in gold, around her neck. $2,000.00.
Photo by Linda Ching

# Storybook Creatures and Characters

*"To me, dolls are natural storytellers. They touch a chord in me that runs straight to my childhood."*

*-Mo'a Romig-Boyles*

Comedy. . .Tragedy? by Mo'a Romig-Boyles.
Measuring 22" and made of Aves Apoxie Sculpt and paperclay, Comedy. . .Tragedy? is garbed in paper and acrylic paints. $950.00.
Photo by Kenneth G. Boyles

## Linnea Polk

Home/Studio ..........Florissant, Missouri
E-mail ....................erpolk@sbcglobal.net
Media .....................Polymer clay, cloth
Dolls' Price Ranges..$60.00 – $120.00
Member..................Artists Boutique

## Wellspring:

"Childhood memories have definitely inspired my creations. My mother told me stories of trolls, witches, gnomes, and fairies. They were wonderful little people, lovers of nature, who did amazing things in the woodlands of Sweden.

"I imagine the little people in my mother's stories could look much like my Flyhoppers™. I am not a storyteller, but I do pick up my dolls on occasion and have them carry on conversations with my grandchildren, through me. It's fun to draw my grandchildren into my world of imagination. When they see my dolls, they will remember these times with me."

## The Legend of the Flyhoppers™: A Retelling of a Made-Up Fairy Tale

Bengt, Birra, and Bror were handsome and hardworking fairy brothers. They lived in a flower garden with all the other fairies. Whispering and laughing, they played all day with the bees and other garden creatures.

They had the chore of dusting the stars each evening just before nightfall. Their stars were said to be the shiniest of all. In their woodland fairy world, Bengt, Birra, and Bror were loved by all.

At night, lighting the way with fireflies, the three brothers would return to the knotholes of their tree homes to sleep.

The fairies were also mischievous. They loved to play jokes, and play them they did on their faithful animal friends. One day, the threesome played their best joke yet on Rainbow Pony. Unfortunately, Rainbow Pony was hurt as a result of the prank.

Word spread swiftly through the woodland and Bengt, Birra and Bror fell from favor. The fairy queen took their fairy bodies from them and gave them new identities: trolls. None of the garden creatures liked the lazy trolls who were always lurking about, waiting to capture the fairies and take them underground to force them to do their chores.

With their new identities, the three brothers were banished from their woodland fairy world and sent to Earth where they were ordered to live forever in the forests of Sweden. In her goodness the fairy queen gave the trio of trolls one chance to redeem themselves; she made Bengt, Birra, and Bror the overseers of all the living creatures in the forests.

Bengt, Birra, and Bror met many other trolls in the forest. Some were very unpleasant, but some were good. They learned to understand the animals and were forever ashamed for their earlier behavior.

To this day the three brothers live as proud protectors of all woodland creatures.

## *The Stuff of Nightmares*

It is a wonder that Linnea Polk didn't have nightmares throughout her childhood. Murderous monarchs, beheadings, and poisonings — such was the stuff of many of the yarns spun by Linnea's mom, Evelyn Llewellyn Mellin, an American who married a Swede and became enamored of the lore of her husband's native Scandinavia.

"Sweden has an abundance of old castles dating back to the twelfth and thirteenth centuries. Some were connected with stories of violence and death, events probably very common in those times. These stories were repeated to me as a child."

Half a century later, Linnea still remembers the substance of some of her mother's tales: "The monarch Eric XIV was said to have been insane. Many people close to him were put to death in dungeons and he was eventually murdered by poison served to him in his soup."

Another bedtime tale featured a royal family, two brothers, one crown, and the removal of an obstacle to the throne: one of the brothers.

"This was a long, long time ago. One brother cut off the head of the other so he could be the next ruler."

Also prominent were Evelyn's forest fantasy stories which featured an assortment of woodland creatures she culled from Sweden's treasure trove of fairy tales and folk tales that harkened back to the oral tradition: slovenly trolls waiting to pounce, good fairies ready to spread their magic, enchanted fireflies moonlighting as lamplighters on dark and scary trails.

Some of the characters resembled the handmade wood and moss troll and fairy type dolls Linnea would receive for birthday and Christmas presents from her Swedish relatives. When those dolls stopped coming, Linnea began making her own dolls.

"These were mostly paper and stick dolls, crude versions of my Swedish dolls, but their influence stayed with me through the years."

Most of Linnea's Flyhoppers™ are about 14" tall and have weighted bottoms for solid seating. Their faces, hands, and feet are sculpted from polymer clay with different colors of Fimo and transparent Sculpey clays mixed for different skin tones. Fabrics and trims are always mixed and matched to achieve costumes evocative of woodlandwear. $60.00 – $120.00.

Two Flyhoppers™ share secrets on a bench. $60.00 – 120.00 each.

A favorite recurring character in Evelyn's tales was the enchanted fairy hero. Oftentimes he was named for Linnea's grandfather, Bengt Gustav Mellin, who had been captain of the guards of the Royal Palace in Stockholm; other times he was called Bror, after Linnea's father.

Like Evelyn, Bror George Mellin sparked his daughter's imagination in the fantasy realm with childhood visits to his homeland. It would be years after taking those treks to Sweden's centuries-old fortresses, cathedrals, and palaces, however, before Linnea would discover a love of doll making that also allowed her to reclaim her mother's legends and folk tales.

"I started making dolls when my first grandchild was born in 1990. Breonna is biracial and I couldn't find anything I really liked as a plaything for her, something she could identify with."

So Linnea made little dolls that looked like her granddaughter, which was like taking the proverbial finger out of the dyke. Linnea's Swedish heritage poured forth with all the long-forgotten fairy tales her mother had told her and into her now trademarked Flyhoppers™.

"Making the dolls took me back to where I started: storytelling, Sweden."

Linnea's Flyhoppers™ are original, one-of-a-kind woodland wonders: enchanted monkeys, bears, and birds, magical jesters, little bewitched beings called Travelers, and endearing trolls. Their faces, hands, and feet are sculpted from polymer clay with different colors of Fimo™ and transparent Sculpey™ clays blended to achieve a variety of skin tones. Their bottoms are filled with copper BBs for solid seating.

Some of the figures hold gilded baubles and miscellaneous bits of "this and that" as accents to their mixmatch garments. All sport the silly, signature ear-to-ear grin that gives their little faces an old-world look, and, with the exception of some of the monkeys, every figure is topped with a hat in the Flyhopper™ tradition.

Their bodies are sewn from fine designer fabrics, many of which Linnea happens upon in various shops while on sailing adventures with her husband, Roger. Every fall, when Roger heads to the boat show in Annapolis, Maryland, Linnea zips over to Alexandria, Baltimore, and Fells Point to shop for decorator fabrics and vintage trinkets.

This Flyhopper™ family is dressed in strips of handdyed gauze that allow the artist to play with color and texture without adding bulk to the bodies. They are gathered on a bench for storytime. $105.00.

Tapestries are reminiscent of old-world décor and are therefore the perfect choice for Linnea's royal jester Flyhoppers™. Floral and island prints in bold greens and yellows bring out the jungle in her monkeys.

Suedes in earth tones and hand-dyed gauzes with accents of dried moss, bark, and nuts enhance her woodland troll themes and resemble the handmade trolls from Sweden that she would receive as gifts. Working with gauze fabric allows Linnea to achieve a playfully layered look without adding bulk to her figures. She then trims them with imported yarns and threads from the shop of a weaver friend and heaps tiny star-shaped moss onto their laps to reflect her woodsy motif.

"Fabric plays a vital role in my doll making because it sets the mood and style of my characters. Fabric helps to tell the story."

Many of these stories that Linnea's characters so richly relate take place in the misty woodlands and very old castles of Sweden. Linnea found the castles, with their huge archways and passageways, secret rooms, dungeons, and grand halls filled with murals, art work, and fine furniture to be magical — just the sort of place where fairytale characters would thrive. Outside, the rock walls, garden paths, and waterways fueled her imagination that little creatures must surely inhabit the area.

"My jester dolls are in the castles. The trolls are hiding in the forest and the birds and monkeys are everywhere. They all have a story to be imagined."

The artist is influenced by everything around her and admits that she changes fabric textures and color choices on a regular basis to create different characters. When she combined richly textured upholstery material with airy drapery fabrics, her tasseled Travelers emerged.

"Another doll artist shared this fabric with me. I played with it and came up with the Travelers. I needed simple construction for rather stiff and full-bodied fabric. These fabrics have so much body to them and many of the weaves look handmade. Now I find dressing my dolls just as creative and fun as sculpting their faces."

Linnea's latest creative impulse led to the creation of fully sculpted birds that wear crowns of flyaway hair and big, silly smiles. They are the gossips of Linnea's growing Flyhopper™ family, flittering among the trolls and sprites like little

❖⟼⟻❖

These Royal Jesters show off Linnea's love of fine fabrics, threads, and trims. $85.00 each.

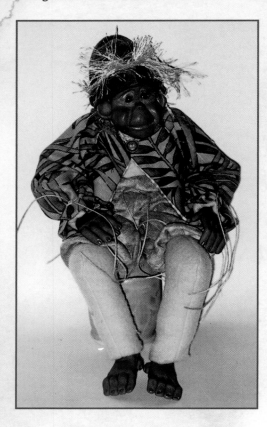

Monkey shows off his jungle prints and trims. $80.00.

fussbudgets. Linnea hand-applies a paint rub to the birds that she discovered in a scrapbook supply shop to achieve their muted yet iridescent skin tones.

"With fantasy folk and animals there is the advantage of creating with no set rules and being in complete control."

Linnea's fantasy forest beings were christened Flyhoppers because the artist's studio windows look out on heavily wooded acreage.

"All day, animals are flying and hopping by. I needed one special word for all my creations: Flyhoppers! The name came from a thought that leapt to my mind while watching all these creatures outside my window. Hopefully, my dolls make people smile and exude a sense of kindness and merriment."

Linnea is a prolific doll maker, turning out sometimes as many as 200 of the little woodland sprites in all their trims and finery each year. Her Flyhoppers™ are sold primarily through galleries and boutiques, as well as at the four fine art festivals she participates in each year in Illinois and Missouri. She has a loyal following of collectors, many of whom own well over a dozen different pieces. She deliberately keeps her prices moderate, tagging the trolls, jesters, Travelers, monkeys, bears, and other fantasy figures to sell quickly in order to make room for new creations.

"I love playing with ideas and I love creating. Each time a Flyhopper™ sells, it's like someone is buying into my world of imagination."

Linnea returned to her mother's stories to share them with her grandchildren, creating the characters that would have been right at home in those tales. A few collectors have told her that her Flyhoppers™ are ugly and creepy, but Linnea is quick to point out that the Swedish tradition of folklore has to do with death, killings, and royalty. Her mother was captivated by it and that in turn enchanted Linnea.

"Through my doll making I keep alive the spirit of imagination, reminiscent of the fantasy and folklore stories I heard as a child."

The Travelers are dressed for an adventure and ready to explore. Donning caps and walking shoes, these tasseled Flyhoppers™ carry pouches to collect souvenirs. $65.00 each.

## Mo'a Romig-Boyles

Home/Studio ..........Medford, New Jersey
E-mail .....................mrboyles@yahoo.com
Website ...................www.aadadoll.org
Media .....................Paper clay, polymer clay, apoxie
　　　　　　　　　　　sculpt, paper, cloth, and various
　　　　　　　　　　　other media such as eggshell,
　　　　　　　　　　　mosses, seaweed and "whatever
　　　　　　　　　　　catches my fancy"
Dolls' Price Ranges..$45.00 – $3,000.00
Member..................Academy of American Doll
　　　　　　　　　　　Artists, Inc.
Museum .................Wenham Museum, Wenham,
　　　　　　　　　　　Massachusetts

### Wellspring:

"The desire to create is a deep desire that drives everything I do, especially my art. Once I start creating I get so caught up in the process and the creative flow that I can forget everything else. I love this feeling; to me, it is like meditation."

## A Night at the Improv

Mo'a Romig-Boyles grew up loving the type of theater that developed in Italy in the sixteenth and seventeenth centuries and was characterized by improvisation and stock characters, often in traditional masks and costumes — the commedia dell'arte.

"Since I was a small child of five, sitting on my father's shoulders watching a commedia dell'arte performance in the center of Reykjavik on Iceland's national holiday, I have been fascinated by the commedia dell'arte. I take every opportunity I have to see a commedia performance."

Although one of her favorite places is the Oriental Theatre in Tivoli in Copenhagen, Denmark, Mo'a has not forgotten her first experience at the commedia dell'arte from her perch on her father's shoulders. Both frightened and fascinated, Mo'a watched the screen behind which an operation was taking place. In front of the screen stood the character, Columbine, screaming and throwing her hands up to her face. Meanwhile, from behind the screen, Pierrot would emerge every now and then to select an oversized tool: a saw, a hammer, or a pair of pliers.

"At the end of the performance, Harlequin, Pierrot, and the doctor came out from behind the screen and that is when I breathed a sigh of relief and was hooked forever."

Those childhood theater outings continue to figure prominently in Mo'a's work, in both masked characters and her anthropomorphic subjects whose animal natures mask their humanity. She loves the aura of mystery that surrounds masks and the element of surprise embodied by them.

At 18" x 8½" tall, The Awakening is made of wood, epoxy sculpt, polymer clay, paper, mosses, and cloth, and is built around a chair. "I find chairs extremely interesting. There are so many versions of this object that is made for one thing alone, and that is to sit in it." $3,000.00.
Photo by Kenneth G. Boyles

◆━◑◐━◆

"Masks can also be frightening because you don't know what is under them and many times they are designed to frighten. Masks for me in my art are many times shorthand for telling the story, or having the viewer make their own story about a particular piece."

## Telling Tales

A fellow doll artist once told Mo'a Romig-Boyles that she wished she could tell stories with her dolls the way Mo'a does with hers.

"I have always used dolls to tell a story with or to tell a story about. It came so naturally to me that I did not know this when I started making dolls. Sometimes the stories I tell with my dolls are very obvious and at other times they ask the viewer to create their own stories."

The Awakening operates on both of these levels. It is an earthy vignette that invites viewers to interpret a personal narrative through their own lens of experience. It is also a scene that expresses Mo'a's sense of sleepwalking through life and then being nudged awake by a force beyond or outside the individual to life's boundless and sometimes unfathomable possibilities.

"One figure sits and the other stands in the back and wakes up the sitting figure with a gentle loving touch while an enchanted elf looks on. They are all creatures of the forest and have a life all their own. We just happened on them and that is why we see them."

Storytelling in Mo'a's homeland of Iceland is as natural as breathing.

"When I was growing up I would hear stories of the hidden people (creatures who reside in cliffs, boulders and hillocks), as well as of elves, trolls, and other supernatural beings, and never questioned their existence. My grandfather's greatest wish was to see one of the hidden people.

"I remember asking him, 'Afi, (the Icelandic word for grandfather), did you see one today?'"

Alfie, a 12" elf perched on a tree stump, could be one of these hidden people. A sweet-tempered brownie who is enchanted by the very scene of which he is a part, Alfie wears a tunic and leggings constructed of variously hued paper. He recalls the little beings of myths and fables thought to perform helpful deeds at night.

Mo'a, a naturalized U.S. citizen for many of the past 40 years, has lived and worked in various parts of the United States, raising her son with husband, Ken, and pursuing cherished hobbies of cooking (and doing so for large crowds), ornamental gardening, and writing. She is an unabashed lover of the arts and feels that, just like her storytelling impulse, her appreciation of literature, music, and theater comes naturally to her.

"My life is filled with art, all kinds of art. In my family there are musicians, writers, poets, painters and actors. We are all consumed by art. My father, in his younger years, was with the Carnegie Symphony in Pittsburgh and was the concert master. My mother was an actress in Iceland and when I was three years old, I was taken to practically every performance of one of her plays. I was practically born into it."

Closeup of Comedy. . .Tragedy? Photo by Kenneth G. Boyles.

Centuries of theater experiences unfold in the paradoxical figure, Comedy. . .Tragedy?, which recalls a form of ancient Greek and Roman theatrical entertainment on which Mo'a based the character after seeing street mimes performing with Indonesian white masks in Canada.

"I remember being so very fascinated with the mimes and their act. They were identically clothed in black and their masks were identical, yet their personalities were so very different.

"I wondered what their faces looked like under the masks and amused myself by speculating that once they took off their masks their faces would look just like the masks only with different expressions. That is also how the name came to me."

Masks are a recurring theme in Mo'a's work. The Mask Maker, a 12" sculpt clothed in silk, was at one time a fierce lion, but after years of donning a human mask has lost most of his feline characteristics. He is old, gray, and balding, and his tail is a small, thin reminder of what he once was. The Mask Maker is also arthritic and has a hump on his back from years of sitting cross-legged, hunched over his tasks.

Mo'a has traveled all over the country and has been able to experience its rich and varied culture and express these impressions in and through her work.

"Wherever I live and travel, one of my greatest joys is to be able to enjoy the museums, galleries, theaters, and other art venues of the area. These experiences have had a great impact on my art.

"I can call up a favorite image and remember it as I saw it: the color, form, smell, and sound. When I read I can do the same thing, giving the story color, sound, and smell. Needless to say, there have been many books that have been tough for me to read."

Currently the vice president of the Academy of American Doll Artists, Inc., Mo'a has been creating dolls since 1978, when Ken enrolled her in a soft sculpture class on a lark. The whim soon gave way to a serious study of doll making, however, and Mo'a was an earnest and open-minded student. Experimenting first with woven cloth doll construction, Mo'a designed dolls with

The Mask Maker is giving His Royal Pride, another one of Mo'a's characters, a choice of a human or a leopard mask for the ball. He is 12" tall and sculpted of Aves Apoxie Sculpt and paperclay. His masks are of paperclay and his clothing is silk. The Mask Maker lives with His Royal Pride and Queen Pride in a private collection. $850.00.
Photo by Kenneth G. Boyles

Aesop is 20" of paper clay, dressed in wool, and carrying an Adirondack basket on his back. He is Mo'a's interpretation of the fox character in the Aesop fable, *The Fox and the Grapes*. The doll currently resides in the Boyles' Adirondack room in their home in New Jersey. $750.00.
Photo by Bruce E. Harding

painted faces of muslin or velveteen, but felt she lacked the necessary sewing skills to create the quality dolls she visualized.

"I have never met a sewing machine that I could handle. They see me coming and resolve to make my life miserable."

She was introduced to the world of sculpting in 1993 by renowned doll artist Robert Keene McKinley. Later, in a class given by John Darcy Noble, Mo'a discovered a technique for making clothing with cloth and paper that substituted glue for the dreaded sewing machine. She felt both liberated and captivated. Then, several years ago she met figurative doll artist Marilyn Radzat at a National Institute of American Doll Artists convention and learned about the pliability and versatility of ProSculpt, a type of polymer clay.

"I have been using ProSculpt ever since and love the expediency of it. I can sculpt a doll, bake it in the oven, and dress it all in a day if I so choose. Lately I have been using Aves Apoxie Sculpt on areas that would be sensitive to breakage."

She generally has a figure in mind before she sits down with her sculpting tools, envisioning the character, its attitude, expression, and story. Her 20" paper clay Aesop, a play on the Aesopian fable, *The Fox and the Grapes*, tells the story exactly as the artist intended, when she set out to sculpt a fox with a specially designed basket of grapes.

"I thought it would be humorous to have a fox get the grapes. I did not feel it would translate as well to have an owl or a cat with a basket and a handful of grapes.

"We used to live in upstate New York and enjoyed visiting the Adirondacks. A friend made the Adirondack basket that is on Aesop's back for me. I gave him his name to lead the viewer to think of the fable."

Mo'a has no set rules when she makes her dolls and frequently, something serendipitous will happen during the sculpting process. The artist always allows herself to fully succumb to the impulse.

"I don't try to fight the feeling, as sometimes a doll has its own mind as to what it likes to become. I have also had a particular piece in mind and with stubborn resolve not listened, and it will not come through no matter how hard I try. It has happened to me when I was almost finished with the piece the way I thought it should be and it refuses me completely only to later have its own way."

Most of Mo'a's dolls fall in the $150.00 to $750.00 price range and can be found in private collections all over the United States, as well as in England, France, Sweden, Spain, and Iceland. Until recently, she focused on anthropomorphic characters in her work, exploring motivational attributes in such characters as regal lions, gentle lambs, comical pigs, charming cats, and learned owls.

"If a person comes away having thought that my anthropomorphic animals show both their animal and human personality, albeit in a surrealistic way, and if the humor in them comes through, I feel I have accomplished what I set out to do."

With each of her dolls, the artist tries to communicate mood, emotion, and integrity of character. In Frog Astaire, a character that seems to bridge the worlds populated by her animal and human figures, Mo'a is able to articulate her sense of whimsy and drama in a three-dimensional conceit.

"I love frogs and have always been fascinated by their shapely long and human-like legs. I thought to myself once, when I was looking at my favorite frog cooling himself in our fish pond at our home in Salem, 'Wow! I bet he is quite the dancer with legs like these. I bet he is quite the Fred Astaire.'"

Fanciful thinking perhaps, but theater at its best for an artist as visual as Mo'a.

"I can find beauty in what seems mundane to other people; the whole world is eye candy to me. I live and breathe art."

Looking every inch the debonair dancer extraordinaire, the silk and velvet clad Frog Astaire is made of Aves Apoxie Sculpt and paperclay and is painted with metallic acrylics.

"When this commission came up I went on the Internet and looked at hundreds of photos of Fred Astaire dancing. The result was that I combined two poses. I did not want him to be dressed in thirties-style garb and tailored my own version of a commedia dell'arte costume for him." $750.00.
Photo by Kenneth G. Boyles

Alfie perches charmingly on a stump that is part of his enchanted (and enchanting) vignette. He is 12" tall, made of polymer clay, and clothed in paper. $550.00.
Photo by Kenneth G. Boyles

Closeup of Frog Astaire.
Photo by Kenneth G. Boyles

## Jamie Williamson

Studio ....................Rochester, New York
E-mail ....................RWilli1007@aol.com
Medium...................Polymer clay
Dolls' Price Ranges ..$5,000.00 – $13,000.00
Member...................Artists United

### *Wellspring:*

"I see inspiration in oil paintings from the fourteenth through seventeenth centuries, especially ones that show children and young women radiating with innocence and joy.

"I get ideas everywhere. I'll pick up beads from a shop in Chicago or a bunch of shells from the beach in Hawaii and think, 'What can I do with this or that?'

"My creative flow comes from a part of me that longs for purity, innocence, honesty, peace, and joy, and I express it through this art form."

### *Embossing Backdrops*

Jamie Williamson gets much of her inspiration for her one-of-a-kind dolls from paintings she sees in different museums. The frames of those paintings, as well as the backdrops of museum statuary, have inspired the artist to add a new dimension to her doll vignettes: embossed panel scenery.

"Visiting museums is one of my favorite things to do. My husband Randy and I were in a museum one day in New York City and I noticed a lot of paintings of Madonna with these ornate frames and many statues that had backdrops. I was working on a mother and child set who looked like royalty at the time and I thought a backdrop would give them the look of a three-dimensional painting and finish the piece perfectly."

Jamie's backdrops are made from ornate framing that she paints and antiques to complement her dolls, customizing embossed wallpapers, paints, and finishes for each doll. The panels are then assembled using hinges so that the end panels rotate to the front to allow the backdrop to stand on its own.

For the backdrop for Red Ridinghood, Jamie created a textured multi-panel forest scene using framable prints she bought in a craft store that featured woodsy scenes and a picture of a wolf tailored in fabric to fit the landscape. She then layered on stains and varnishes, as well as her own artistic flourishes.

"I also applied several different finishes until I achieved the look I wanted. I even used a crackle finish so the prints would look really old."

Jamie's embossed panel backdrops add one more creative dimension to the artist's doll making process.

"Now I don't even feel my dolls are finished until they have a backdrop."

## Once Upon a Costume

Escape.

This is the word that most perfectly describes what Jamie Williamson feels when she is sculpting.

Escape to a "once upon a time" world of beautiful damsels with intricately dressed hair and graciously attired in sumptuous gowns. Escape to the storybook lands of Cinderella, Rapunzel, Snow White, and Sleeping Beauty.

Fabled young ladies, impeccably coiffed and accessorized and flawlessly costumed in gilt-trimmed raiment and wearing royal, jewel-encrusted headpieces have always held a special fascination for the doll maker.

"Many of my dolls do tend to have a fairytale quality to them, although not intentionally. I'll see a piece of antique lace, some wonderful beaded trim, or a new vibrant shade of raw silk and my mind starts imagining all sorts of costuming possibilities and the beautiful dolls that will wear them."

Jamie's fanciful thinking is apparent in the intricately designed ensembles she fashions for each of her one-of-a-kind, polymer clay dolls. Reference books like *Paintings in the National Gallery London* and *Victorian Painting* are sources of further inspiration on period costuming, as is her collection of Renaissance paintings. She also thumbs through her books of photographs of international photojournalist Steve McCurry.

"I really admire the look of Renaissance costuming with the beautiful sweeping skirts and the beaded head-pieces over long, flowing hair and I love costuming my dolls in Victorian-inspired ensembles."

Jamie's Victorian Child, measuring a substantial 30" tall from beribboned boater to sculpted, leather-look button-up boots, appears the part in her silk full-skirted dress and coat with antique ribbon trims. The jewel tones of Victorian Child's outfit shimmer in sharp contrast to her delicately pale complexion. The little girl embraces a layered-in-lace antique doll and perches on a cushioned pedestal upholstered in an eye-catching safari-print cloth. An embossed background of royal gold and brown adds drama to the overall color scheme.

"I worked for days and days on Victorian Child's dress. I wanted to do a dress authentic to the Victorian period and their clothes were so fussy then."

Just for the doll's leggings, Jamie had to first shape and mold the legs and then the boots which included a sculpted lip around the top. The leggings were put on the doll last, tucked into the lip of each boot and then hand-sewn up the back with painstakingly perfect stitches.

The 30" Victorian Child wears a silk ensemble with stretch-knit leggings and sculpted boots and sits before an embossed panel backdrop. She holds an antique cloth doll. $5,400.00.

Looking as though she belongs in the same era as Victorian Child is Isabella, a fragile beauty dressed in an ice-blue gown that matches the shade of her eyes. Off-the-shoulder sleeves feature a unique crisscross design in a delicate silver thread fabric that Jamie fell in love with at a shop in New York City. She stands 28" tall and has a luxurious crown of copper-colored curls that is encircled by a glittering tiara.

"I love making the costumes. I have so many old, beaded trims that just work perfectly for these dolls."

Jamie discovered one-of-a-kind dolls quite by accident in the mid-1990s when she picked up a ball of polymer clay one morning that had been mysteriously left on her kitchen counter. Working with the clay took Jamie 12 long hours, but by the time night had fallen, the self-taught artist had sculpted her first doll. In the process, Jamie discovered that she had a natural talent for sculpting and was particularly gifted in molding gracefully curved hands and slender fingers. With one look at the finished piece, Jamie knew that her doll, once dressed in the kind of elaborate costumes and headpieces she adored from her books, was the beginning of a new and extraordinary career.

More than ten years and dozens of original dolls later, the lifelong sewer, painter, and potter is ensconced comfortably in her doll making studio, a renovated 120-year-old barn with sun-welcoming 60-foot ceilings. Equipped with a standard-sized digital wall oven and enough countertops to hold her sewing machine, sculpting accouterments, and assorted doll body parts, the studio is "happily ever after" for Jamie, the place where she is free to create to her heart's content.

Each doll is constructed over a three- to four-week period. Jamie works from her imagination, allowing each doll to simply emerge beneath her hands and tools and present her face and personality. Before the sculpts are finished, Jamie has planned her line of couture, selecting all fabrics, trims, accessories, and, most recently, backdrops.

"The panel kind of gives the doll the look of a three-dimensional painting. I feel it finishes the piece perfectly."

Seated before a three-panel woodsy backdrop is one of the artist's favorite pieces: Red Ridinghood. Jamie constructed the backdrop, taking special pains to find a fabric that would colorfully illustrate a Big Bad Wolf lurking behind a tree yonder in the distance. Seemingly unaware of the wolf, Red Ridinghood, looking very smart in her hood trimmed with beading and braiding, tenderly holds Granny's well-stocked basket in the crook of her arm. She sits quietly, the yards of crimson silk forming a train about her legs, from beneath which peeks one finely arched foot.

Each of Jamie's ensembles is enthusiastically detailed with lavish trims of jewels, beads, ribbons, and threads, many of them found on buying trips in New York, Chicago, and Washington, D.C. and quite a few imported from India. Wardrobes include complementary and custom-made hair bows, bonnets, caps, crowns, and other millinery. Antique trims accent some of her costumes and hand-smocking embellishes others. Jamie favors raw silk for gowns because of its lightweight versatility and endlessly hued color palette, and amasses yards of it on her annual shopping trips to New York City's fabled fabric district.

❖➤═◯═◀❖

Isabella, a 28" tall beauty owned by Richard Simmons, is swathed in an ice-blue raw silk gown that matches the shade of her eyes. Jamie loved working with the fussy, open-weave fabric for Isabella's sleeves, made from a favorite fabric she bought in New York City. $5,400.00.

For her cherubic Little Princess, Jamie fashioned a sparkling tiara with a floral motif that is repeated in the neckline of her blue silk frock. The sleeves of the gown are puffed at the upper arms where a beaded floral pattern harmonizes in sweet symmetry with the other design components of the ensemble. Burgundy ribbons provide accents at shoulder and waist and a white tulle overskirt completes the detailing of this extravagant costume.

In her two-generation set entitled Royal Love, Jamie designed elaborate gemstone-encrusted cream silk gowns for the dolls who look more like two czarinas than mother and daughter. She accented the bodice and waistline of the mother's gown with beaded trims. Both dolls are royally fitted with snug beaded caps framed in silver curlicues. The effect is both arresting and charming.

The artist's playfulness comes out in her cast of little girl characters, including pint-size femmes dressed in pirate togs and tutus. Her Ballerina is a serious little miss holding the barre before which she spends so many hours practicing her ballet steps. Her extravagantly embroidered tutu is balanced with a jeweled crown that can't quite contain her erratic curls.

The very embodiment of her moniker, Sour Puss is pure pouty glamour with her antique tulle-edged frock with matching bloomers. Jamie is captivated by these tutued creatures and loves to explore the different facial gestures that her little dancers might express.

Looking as though she just slipped away from a painting by Italian master Raphael, angelic Little Princess wears a raw silk dress and a tiara of rhinestones. "I get so much inspiration from my museum books," says Jamie. $5,200.00.

Although she gets many of her ideas from paintings and pictures in museums and books, when Jamie sits down at her work table she sculpts from everything inside her so that by the end of the sculpting process, the dolls will have become composites of everything the artist has seen and touched. As she works, Jamie lays fabrics and finishes together and "kind of makes things up" as she goes along, intuiting when each piece is completed.

"If I can look at a doll and feel totally peaceful about it, I know it's totally done and I can let it go."

For Jamie, the process of sculpting is a journey to a land of make-believe where returning to reality can be such a challenge, particularly if she is at work on a doll's head, that she has to set time guidelines for herself.

"If I didn't, my kids would never get fed dinner! When I sculpt, I am somewhere else. I simply escape into my work and it is a feeling of total peace for me.

Jamie's work is so much a part of her that she literally longs for it when she is away from it, even when taking a well-deserved vacation.

"My work completes me in a way I can't even put into words."

There really is no need for Jamie to articulate what her work means to her; her storybook dolls speak volumes about the artist — and her art.

Royal Love features two blonde, blue-eyed beauties wearing cream silk designer fabrics with beaded trims and head-pieces finished with beading from India. The set includes an ornate footstool Jamie made from an old box unearthed at an antique store and a backdrop made with embossed wallpaper. $13,000.00.

Sour Puss has German glass eyes and unruly red mohair wig. Her outfit is made of silk with antique trims. $5,000.00.

Red Ridinghood has human hair and German glass eyes. Her dress and cape are made of silks with antique trims. A backdrop featuring a woodsy scene — complete with Big Bad Wolf — completes the vignette. This is the artist's favorite piece. $8,400.00.

# September 11

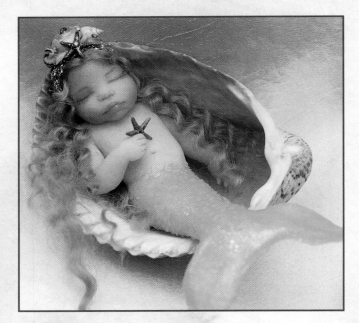

"*I wanted something to symbolize my memory of my sister and I wanted to pursue my art because she loved my art. That's how Forget Me Not fairy was born.*"

*-Kim Jelley*

Sea Siren and Little Seamaiden by Kim Jelley. Little Seamaiden is sweetly snuggled with her tiny starfish into her comfy shell cradle for a nap. At just 5½", she fits comfortably in the palm of your hand. Her hair is adorned with tiny treasures from the sea. $450.00.
Photo by Kim Jelley

Curvaceous Sea Siren beckons with beautiful green glass eyes and hand-applied eyelashes. Measuring approximately 7" high by 7½" wide by 7" deep, this fantasy figure crowned with hand-made tiara sprinkled with real starfish and vintage crystals is fully armatured and has wavy, long brown mohair sparked with blond highlights. She has an interchangeable shell necklace that can be flipped around to her back to reveal a flower choker necklace. The shells were hand sculpted and her silver tail has hundreds of miniature scales meticulously hand-sculpted one at a time. $1,200.00.
Photo by Kim Jelley

## Jean Bernard

Home/Studio............Reno, Nevada
E-mail.......................jean@bernard-dolls.com
Website .....................www.bernard-dolls.com
Media ........................Polymer clay and epoxy sculpt
Dolls' Price Ranges..$500.00 – $2,000.00
Member ....................Academy of American Doll Artists, Inc.

### Wellspring:

"God and life – that's where my inspiration comes from and from, all the simple qualities like love and tenderness that I think we're lacking. I'm not materialistic; I'm a hippie from the old days and I feel we need to get back to basics.

"When I make a piece, what comes out of me is not from me, it's my higher power. It's all God's hand at work. I like to say, 'Look what God and I did today!'"

### On September 11

"September 11 forever changed the world and my perspective of it. It caused me to open my eyes, my mind, and, most of all, my heart. I, like so many Americans prior to September 11, was oblivious to my everyday encounters and surroundings. The world's pace had sped up tenfold and the true meaning of life had been forgotten.

"I think the September 11 tragedy caused us as a nation to unite and finally feel for the first time in decades. Love, trust, respect, and kindness to our fellow man was not something we practiced on a daily basis. For a brief time after the tragedy, the world came together as one. The simplistic lifestyle was practiced. Priorities changed. Helping hands were extended. 'Self' was removed from the picture for a brief moment in time and love and compassion ran rampant throughout the world."

### Guiding the Lost to Heaven

For Jean Bernard, life's true meaning revealed itself in six pounds of clay that eventually became a regal figure reminiscent of Lady Liberty. Christened Stairway to Heaven, the 19" one-of-a-kind doll wears a hand-carved tiara and the gloss of bronzed paint and highlights.

## Footprints in the Sand
by Mary Stevenson*

One night I dreamed I was walking
Along the beach with the Lord.
Many scenes from my life flashed across the sky.
In each scene I noticed footprints in the sand.
Sometimes there were two sets of footprints.
Other times there was one set of footprints.
This bothered me because I noticed that
During the low periods of my life when I was
Suffering from anguish, sorrow, or defeat,
I could see only one set of footprints,
So I said to the Lord, "You promised me,
Lord, that if I followed You,
You would walk with me always.
But I noticed that during the most trying periods
Of my life there have only been
One set of prints in the sand.
Why, When I have needed You most,
You have not been there for me?"
The Lord replied,
"The times when you have seen only one set of footprints
Is when I carried you."

*This verse was copyrighted in 1984 by Mary Stevenson who originally wrote it in 1936. There is another version, *I Had a Dream/Footprints in the Sand*, written by Margaret Fishback Powers in 1964 and copyrighted in 1987. When *Footprints in the Sand* first appeared in print, it was credited to Author Anonymous.

"The September 11 tragedy was a huge turning point for me. As painful as the whole event was, I truly believe it had a positive outcome as well. It seemed to remind everyone that it is time to get back to the basics and enjoy the true meaning of life. For me, that would be one of the greatest gifts we can give to the ones that perished on that awful day in September."

Jean sought truth at the end of her fingertips as she fashioned beauty and harmony from polymer clay, constructing a full-body sculpt over a tinfoil core. Stairway to Heaven wears the wings of angels and, like a mother cuddling her newborn, hugs an American flag to her chest. A lace-embossed dress is pleated with 70 steps that form a path to guide all those lost on September 11 to heaven.

"Going through the process of individually sculpting each step allowed me to focus on each person who lost his or her life on that tragic day."

A self-proclaimed hippy, Jean entered the world of doll making just five years ago after working nearly 11 stressed-out years as an administrative assistant at an 80-attorney law firm. Shortly after she bade farewell to the corporate world, Jean's mother- and father-in-law gave her a 50-year-old cloth snowman that had been given to them as a gift by her husband's grandmother. The beloved doll was sorely in need of restoration work and Jean heartily took up the challenge. Repairing the snowman launched her directly into doll making.

"I was always fixing things and I think I was creating before I was even conceived. I always seemed to surround myself with creative things to do."

Jean credits her Japanese heritage for her artistic side. Born in Osaka, Japan, to a Japanese mother and an American G.I. father, Jean sees the spirituality and simplicity of Japanese culture in her work, even though her family moved to the United States when she was three.

Even as a child, Jean would raid her mother's kitchen garbage can and smuggle the treasures outside. She would then sculpt items like eggs, pancakes, and bacon, usually from mud, to fill in the empty containers.

"I played with many dolls but I always gave them a makeover: cutting their hair, applying makeup, designing fancy dresses and hairpieces. I liked to play with paper dolls a lot too. I made all their clothes and even made paper furniture for them."

Once Jean rediscovered her love of sculpting she began researching clays, ultimately settling on polymer clay because of its versatility. She also read books by Jack Johnston, a leading expert in sculpting art dolls, and took a sculpting class with him. She followed that up with a doll making workshop with baby doll artist Pat Moulton. Both encouraged Jean to continue her studies and her sculpting. She began devouring anatomy books and became an ardent people watcher.

"I would stare at men's and women's faces, but pretty soon I stopped staring at the men's faces because the women were getting ticked off!"

Today Jean's work appears in private collections all over the world. Each piece reflects Jean's artistic journey and every doll always includes some hidden design element, the artist's signature flourish, such as beading and undergarments.

"Socks, stockings, lining, slips, camisoles, belts, waistbands, decorative lace backs — things that I know are there but will never be seen by the collector — give each of my pieces an overall finished feel.

"I don't skimp just because you can't see the details I put into the work. The hidden surprises may never be seen but if one lifts a particular piece of clothing, shades of the surprise will appear."

With the sculpting of Stairway to Heaven, Jean also learned a valuable lesson about her art: "Each piece should be made from deep inside the artistic soul, not for money, not for consumers, but for oneself. I made this piece because it helped me heal.

"You learn the basics of sculpting, take all you can from instructors' books. Once you figure out the process, then you take what's in your heart and soul and put it into a piece that reflects your personality.

"If you put your hand over heart, it's always the right hand. On Stairway to Heaven, I have the figure's left hand over her heart. When you're in a moment of shock and hurt, as we were on September 11, you cradle yourself. I noticed when I was creating her that my left hand would go over my heart. That was an emotional gesture on my part." This full-body sculpt weights six pounds and has a bronze sheen, clutches an American flag, and has intricately detailed wings that were made with two sets of wings pressed together to give the illusion of flow. $1,200.00.

A rear view of Stairway to Heaven reveals the hole the artist deliberately left in the figure's head. "This is the portal to heaven for those lost that tragic day."

You put yourself into it. That, I think, is when the true artist comes out and when the piece speaks to you, but you have to go through the process of learning the anatomy, of learning your skill. Boy, that's when things get really exciting."

Jeans admits that for a time following the September 11 tragedy, she was so grief stricken, shocked, and ashamed that she was unable to do the one thing she loves the most: sculpt. Days bled one into the next and eventually Jean realized she would have to find an outlet for all her emotions. She began sketching her feelings onto paper and came up with a draft of what would become Stairway to Heaven.

"I began sculpting not realizing which directions my hands would take me. I did not intend for the piece to look like an angel and the Statue of Liberty."

Following her hands, Jean began forming steps and realized that the figure's staircase design would play an integral part in articulating her vision of guiding all the lost souls to heaven. Fixed firmly in her mind were the words of Mary Stevenson's poem, *Footprints in the Sand*, particularly the line, "The times when you have seen only one set of footprints/Is when I carried you." During the sculpting process, Jean would get so lost in the design that untold hours would slip by. When she finally stopped sculpting she would be mentally, physically and spiritually drained.

"This piece is truly full of my emotions and it shows. It helped me heal and that is why I made her."

It also reminded her that hope could stay alive even in the midst of heartbreaking tragedy.

"I injected a bit of humor into this piece. It was therapeutic. She has underwear on that you can't see, but they're there. I just feel that there truly is hope for us if we can hang onto our humor."

Besides Stairway to Heaven, Jean has sculpted numerous dolls, all containing hidden flourishes, including a fantasy piece named Conquering Demons, which features a mermaid sitting on a snail and holding a dragon's head in her hand. Created in recognition of the demons she has conquered, the doll boasts 40 hours worth of lavish hand-applied beading: Australian crystals and glass beads and seeds, all in golds and shades of brown.

Another figure is called Mother. "She's half mother and, from the waist down, half tree. There are children inside the root system. The children's hair turns into limbs and branches. One child's knee and leg appears to be a tree trunk but in fact is a knee and leg. I do not intentionally do this — it just happens."

The artist hopes that collectors will see something new and different each time they look at one of her pieces. She describes a chair she fashioned for a 10" baby doll named Edwina that includes 6" to 8" green and gold leaves made of polymer clay jutting from the back of the chair: "The chair legs look like twisted branches — yes, I do love trees! — but if you look real close, the left leg is actually a dragon's head and

*⊷═◦═⊶*

Jewels is a 19" polymer clay mermaid costumed in a small fortune of glass beads and crystals. With synthetic braided wig and hand-painted eyes, Jewels sparkles from her perch upon a snail that is part serpent and given a tortoise-shell effect. The snail wears a hand-beaded collar and is fitted with a gold harness layered with thousands of gold glass beads to resemble algae and water bubbles. $1,200.00.

the right leg is the dragon's claw." Beneath the chair seat is a tree branch that is also a dragon's body whose tail swoops out the back of the chair. Jean carefully textured the bottom half of the chair to look like dragon scales; from a distance, however, it looks like a tree.

"Art can be pretty basic and typical, but I love to take it a level or two higher. My work is not simply what it appears to be."

Made of polymer clay, sweet-faced Edwina wears a tan and gold jumper adorned with scads of glass beads. Her red-gold hair is of mohair and her eyes are a vivid hand-painted green. This fantasy piece measures 10" and boasts the artist's signature flourish: a hidden surprise is discovered in the chair, the bottom of which looks like a tree but is actually a sweet-natured dragon resting beneath the seat. Edwinda the doll is $395.00; the chair is $185.00.

The Gold Chair, also known as The Rising Sun, is a self-portrait of the artist that reflects Jean's Japanese heritage. She also sculpted a sun onto the chair to symbolize the Japanese flag which depicts a rising sun. Near the left side of Jean's portrait is a cave-like opening through the chair; on the back side of the chair is a flowing river and waterfall running down the length of the chair and surrounded by a bamboo forest. The water symbols represent the artist's tears of joy. $385.00.

Mother is a 23" full-body fantasy piece made of polymer clay and Aves Apoxie Sculpt. The upper portion of Mother's body is garbed in moss green and copper-colored silk; the bottom portion is a sienna-shaded sculpt featuring children carved into it. Jean trimmed the piece with thousands of tiny glass beads to resemble dewdrops. $995.00.

Closeup of Mother's trunk. The piece is very detailed. Jean explains: "The upper portion is sculpted with the human anatomy in mind. The lower portion resembles a tree. Three children are at play amongst the tree trunk and branches. The children's hair, arms, and legs fade into the tree's components. Mother was made to reflect the birth of mankind."

## Kim Jelley

Studio ....................Bay Shore, New York
E-mail ....................kimjelley@hotmail.com
Website ..................www.theartistdoll.com/kimjelley.html
Media .....................Polymer clay and resin
Doll's Price Ranges ..$149.00 – $2,500.00
Member..................Academy of American Doll Artists, Inc.

## *Wellspring:*

"As an artist, I have to create. I've done different things and explored different media like drawing and painting. The most fulfilled I've ever felt was when I created something from within me, not something I saw. It's coming from within me; whatever that 'it' is, it's coming out. I'm able to look at something and interpret and it kind of comes out of me in a form.

"Whenever I go into that creative trance, it takes over. I'm not copying anyone's style. I'm not influenced by anyone and I'm happy about that. I never took classes by any of the doll artists, not because I don't want to, but because I don't want to sculpt under others' influences. I'm happy my work is different. It's unique. It's my own interpretation, my own style. I may see something that inspires me, but I put my own part of me into it.

"Creating dolls is an incredible journey of self-expression and neverending challenge. I feel most at home with my hands in the clay and hope this wonderful doll making journey never ends."

## *In a New York Second, Everything Changed*

"After September 11, it was questionable that I would ever want to or could create again. One of the things that pushed me on was the fact that my sister would never want me to stop with my art. I'm still dealing with major depression and even though I am now able to create again, those little moments of joy are soon over-shadowed by the grim reality that my sister is not here to enjoy my art with me. I am still having a very rough time accepting that I will never hear or see her again. She was my greatest fan of my art. She would be the very first person I would say, 'Sis, you have got to see my latest fairy!' I try to remind myself that she is with me in spirit, but it is not the same, nor is it enough.

"Needless to say, I'm not the same person I was before September 11. One positive thing that changed was that I put my priorities in the right place: my health, my family, my art. It used to be art, family, and my health,

Kim Jelley and her sister, Michelle Titolo.

which is never a good thing. I'm taking better care of myself now. The other positive thing that I realized is that life is precious, unpredictable, and short. I appreciate that God gave me a gift and I feel obligated to express it as long as I am able to."

## Flower Lore

All flowers articulate a message. Roses and tulips, for instance, tell tales of love. Daisies speak of innocence; irises of passion; and lilies of purity.

In the language of flowers, the message of the delicate forget-me-not is obvious: Always remember. Indeed, in *The Language of Flowers, Symbols and Myths* (Prestel Verlag, 2001), writer Marina Heilmeyer notes that forget-me-not's "very name tells us that it has come to signify human longing for loyalty and lastingness."

After Kim Jelley lost her sister, Michelle Titolo, she decided to create a memorial in a garden setting that would include forget-me-not flowers.

"One of the things that has and always will be very painful is that there is no grave for my sister as her body was never recovered. Losing someone is always difficult, but never being able to recover their body adds so much more pain and torment to an already horrible situation. Forever classified as 'missing and presumed dead' somehow seems to leave the wounds open, preventing closure."

The centerpiece of Kim's garden memorial is an angel wearing a locket that holds a picture of her sister. Kim planted a bleeding heart bush and masses of forget-me-nots and pansies, which were Michelle's favorite flower. Pansies are the perfect accompaniment for the forget-me-nots for in the language of flowers they symbolize thoughtfulness and keeping another always in one's thoughts.

## Forget Me Not

A Marilyn Monroe look-alike captured in miniature in all her pouty-lipped sexuality and with a price tag of $2,500.00. An oh-so-svelte mermaid shimmering in an iridescent silver tail — an absolute steal at $450.00. A delicate fairy with removable hand-crafted tiara encrusted with brilliant amber Swarovski crystals priced (and purchased) at $925.00.

The garden memorial Kim designed in her Long Island backyard to honor the memory of her sister.

The theme of Forget-Me-Not is that the artist will never forget her sister. Kim wanted the fairy to convey the idea that the memory of Michelle Titolo will live on forever. "I wanted Forget-Me-Not to have an expression of wistfulness and of thought — holding all the memories of my sister. The flowers in her hand are a symbol of those memories." In private collection.

Kim Jelley's career as a fine art doll artist was just beginning to take off after four years of sculpting exquisitely detailed mermaids, fairies and other exotic beauties when her world imploded. Kim's only sibling, 34-year-old Michelle Titolo, an employee at Cantor Fitzgerald in New York City, was killed in the September 11 tragedy.

"To say the least, losing my precious sister was a horrific loss. She was my only sibling. We were extremely close and only four years apart."

A lifelong learner, Michelle had earned her Master's degree in Business Administration in January of 2001. With her new degree and new job as Assistant ITD Equity Controller at Cantor Fitzgerald, Michelle was thrilled about the direction in which her life was moving. She was known among family and friends for her dedication to her studies, her generosity and warmth, and her love of sappy ballads and disco music.

"Michelle loved England, loved tea. She loved playing pool, drinking Bass beer, and hanging out with her buddies after a long week. She worked hard and played hard. She was a real people person and would always hug and kiss everyone hello and goodbye.

"We were so close, almost like twins. We had the same mannerisms and similar voices. We even had the same callous on the same finger! She was my little shadow, always following me around when we were kids — my little sis who always looked up to me."

She had also always been Kim's most enthusiastic supporter when it came to her art. It was Michelle to whom Kim would turn not only for approval on a certain piece of sculpture but for the sheer joy of sharing her own excitement about a new doll and having it reciprocated by her equally delighted sister.

After losing Michelle in the September 11 attack, Kim was overwhelmed with grief and found she was unable to sculpt. Months passed and the condition remained unchanged. She developed a herniated disc in her neck due to the stress related to her loss and shock. It was a condition that would last over three months, effectively immobilizing her. Six months later, when Kim was finally able to sculpt again, her first creation was a memorial to her sister.

"It is a Forget-me-not fairy, which I feel is very fitting for how I feel about my beloved sister — that I will never forget her. This little fairy was quite a lot of work, as I used real forget-me-not flowers that I grew in my backyard. She has dozens and dozens of them all over her dress and her flower cap. She is even holding a tiny bouquet of forget-me-nots in her hand."

A self-taught artist who worked in charcoals before taking up sculpting tools, Kim plans to eventually

The piece explores concepts of origin, freedom, and life beyond earth, among other topics.

"The more I think about it the more I realize why I did the alien piece. I have a natural ability to heal others and I naturally tried to heal myself in ways I wasn't completely aware of at the time I was sculpting The Promise."

Karen wants The Promise to help heal others and hopes the sculpture speaks for all the unfulfilled promises made in the names of the children who were lost September 11 and for those lost to their parents all through time.

"I believe that a loving heavenly Father sent angels to meet those lost on September 11. He would not allow innocent souls to wonder unhappy and alone at any of the 9-11 sites.

"God keeps his promises even when we cannot. And I believe he kept his promise to love us always and to bring us home."

With 7" of sculpted child suspended in liquid in a bottle that is covered in colorful glass mosaic, Atlantis (Alien in a Bottle) was made by the artist to provoke conversation. The aliens have glass bodies and resin heads; all of the figures, including the child, have Swarovski crystals and genuine opals on their heads. The sand and the plant in the bottle glow in the dark.

"Perhaps someday we will leave Earth and make a new colony on a distant planet where we will learn to live in peace. After many millennia, the inhabitants may consider replanting earth with a new partial human being. The creatures in my piece are discussing whether or not to send the child they created home to Earth." $2,200.00.

Commemorating the lost pilots of September 11 and the lost crew of the Columbia shuttle disaster is Wings. The piece measures 23" tall x 11" wide and includes a 5" polymer clay fairy sitting in the branches of natural manzanita which are trimmed with beads and crystals. "Our dreams of the future start when we are young. The fairy sits unafraid on the edge of her nest; likewise, people who love flying are also not afraid of the dangers of their profession." $1,100.00.

# Christmastide

"*Each of our Santas takes on its own personality. We hope that people see the love and attention that has gone into each of our Santa figures.*"

*-Cheryl and Deanna Brenner*

Barnett by Cheryl Brenner and Jameson by Deanna Brenner. Barnett stands 22" and wears an old wool coat cut down and trimmed in fur. He carries lots of gifts, including the beloved children's book, *Frog and Toad*, as well as a character from the story, plus a wooden doll, nutcracker, and teddy bear. $350.00.
Photo by Larry Lauszus

30" Jameson is a Safari Santa bundled in white fleece and suede boots. He carries a staff and totes a hodgepodge of African accessories, including a metal African mask, wooden marionettes depicting Monkey See, Monkey Hear, and Monkey Do, greenery, wooden ornaments, and a tiny giraffe and elephant. $400.00.
Photo by Larry Lauszus

## Cheryl and Deanna Brenner

Studio .....................Newcastle, California
E-mail .....................original@psyber.com
                                deanna@cddolls.com
Website ..................www.cddolls.com
Medium..................Polymer clay
Dolls' Price Ranges ..$85.00 – $1,600.00

## *Wellspring:*

Cheryl: "I have always loved to create with my hands and I found that clay was a wonderful way to express myself. My father, grandmother and high school art teacher have always been very supportive of me in my artistic ability. Even when I was very young, my dad and grandmother showed me all different kinds of media. Once I reached high school, my art teacher turned me on to ceramics and I've been hooked ever since."

"I'm a people watcher. I love to watch a crowd of people and check out their faces. I'll see a great nose or a happy smile and try to create it. Sometimes at doll shows if I see a great jolly face, I'll sculpt the face on the spot. I've taken a lot of figure drawing classes so I have studied the human body, which helps."

Deanna: "I love Christmas. I love to research old Victorian Christmas cards and antique Santas for inspiration. It is so much fun to learn about the history of Santa Claus, St. Nicholas, and Father Christmas. They each have a specific role and they each dress differently, depending on which country they are from and their time in history.

"I might find a great treasure or perhaps a beautiful piece of antique fabric and I can just imagine what kind of Santa that I can create from it. I love finding antiques from different countries, such as German tin toys, wooden shoes from Holland, and tapestries from Belgium. Then I know that I want to make an Old World Santa.

"Like Cheryl, I'm a people watcher. If I see someone who has a certain look, maybe a great nose or shape of mouth, I try to remember and recreate that same look while I am sculpting. I also may come across an old photo and try and reproduce it in clay. A few of my Santas definitely resemble my relatives."

## *The Legend of La Befana*

There are many versions of the legend of La Befana (the Italian "gift giver"), a favorite subject to sculpt for both Cheryl and Deanna Brenner. One popular rendition is that the Three Kings, en route to see the Christ child, stopped at La Befana's home on their way to Bethlehem. They dined with her and then invited her to join them in their journey, but she refused in order to wash and clean up after dinner.

At some point in the evening, La Befana changed her mind and decided to join the Three Kings. Gathering up some gifts for the Christ child, she set out to find the Three Kings, but she could find neither them nor the babe. She continues searching even today. Consequently, on the eve of January 5 and the morning of January 6, she visits the children of Italy to fill their stockings with sweet, curly candy if they have been good and with lumps of black coal if they have been bad.

La Befana is both mysterious and old-fashioned, yet children in different parts of the world still wait for the dear old woman to pay them a call on her holiday, the Epiphany.

# Santa Sisters

Cheryl Brenner still fondly remembers waking up one Christmas morning as a child and finding what would be her most prized gift from Santa Claus: her first Hot Wheels set.

"I was so excited! There were only boys who lived on my block. They all came over and we set up the track in the driveway."

Oddly enough, the woman who today sculpts up to 50 dolls a year never played with dolls as a child and finds it hilarious that she now makes dolls for a living. But her sister-in-law, Deanna Brenner, loved dolls; her most cherished childhood Christmas present was a little blond-haired doll given to her by her grandmother. She also loved to play with dolls.

"My favorite thing to do was to set up my chalkboard and pretend that I was their school teacher. I would set my dolls all in a row so that they were listening to me teach."

Those dolls are boxed up and packed away now, but Deanna still spends much of her time in the company of dolls. Like Cheryl, Deanna makes up to 50 dolls a year, the majority of which are Santa Claus, Father Time, Le Befana, Belsnickle, and Old World St. Nicholas figures. And the Brenners spend much of their time in each other's company — more than most sisters do, but just enough time for the two sisters-in-law, who say they were destined to be "soul mates."

Cheryl and Deanna met as seventh grade school girls in a California classroom and became fast friends. They dated one set of brothers in high school and married a different set, the brothers Brenner, after a few years of college. They have lived within shouting distance of each other almost since the last handful of rice was thrown at their weddings.

Emma is a 30" La Befana. She is dressed for her neverending sojourn in a hooded velvet cloak trimmed in mink. The white-haired giver of gifts is laden with toys, books, and fruits for good boys and girls. For naughty children, Emma is ready with a tiny bucket of coal. $325.00.

"We have been best friends, business partners, and next door neighbors for years and years."

Nearly ten years ago, Cheryl and Deanna saw a picture of a sculpted Santa Claus in a magazine and decided they would create their own. Both have artistic backgrounds. Cheryl was a ceramics major in college where she honed her future sculpting skills; Deanna, a marine biology major, always dabbled in one art form or another. Both are also huge fans of everything Christmas and share a particular affection for jolly old St. Nick. Sculpting Santas together suited both perfectly.

Says Deanna: "Living so close to each other works out great for us. We each do our own dolls, but we often ask each other for advice or help on a project."

Each Brenner Santa is an original creation, hand-sculpted in polymer clay and signed, dated, and numbered by the artist. Cheryl and Deanna have extensively researched the history of Christmas, traced Santa's origins in dozens of countries, and studied the traditions, customs, and lore specific to those countries. All of these insights are evident in each twinkling eye, each merry dimple, and every tailor-made costume and hand-picked selection of accessories and trims.

Deanna's Dietrich is an Old World Santa suited up in vintage silk and velvet quilting with plush fur trim.

He wears a generous white beard beneath his droll little mouth and is fitted with wooden shoes from Holland. He carries old-fashioned toys in miniature: a doll, a brass horn, a teddy bear, and a sailboat. In one hand, he holds a strand of gold beads and in the other, a red Christmas bell.

Penrod is Cheryl's Belsnickle, the stately fur-trimmed gent popular in eighteenth and nineteenth century Germany. With snowshoes slung over his back and looking very natty in his striped and nubby upholstery fabric, offset by chocolate brown wool cuffs and a flowing white angora beard, Penrod is every ounce the elegant Father Time.

The sisters-in-law routinely use old quilts, coats, and vintage fabrics and embellishments for costuming. Deanna admits that the two haunt the local antique market during show season, buying up suede moccasins and fur coats to cut down for their costumes. They also buy hand-made leather and hand-carved wooden shoes from different sources all over the world.

Finding the best and most appropriate accessories is one of the most challenging aspects of sculpting their Santa dolls — particularly for Deanna whose habit is to envision the entire piece down to theme, trims, and treasures. Once Cheryl and Deanna have an image of the type of Santa they will create next, the two doll makers hit the antique trail.

"We have just as much fun collecting things for our Santas as we do making them," says Cheryl. "I still love the name one of our good friends gave us: Dumpster Divers. It makes me smile because one woman's garbage is another woman's treasure."

The fruits of their labors are seen in the cornucopia of toys, trinkets, and ornaments gathered in the arms and adorning the costumes of their Santa figures. Miniature wooden toys, tiny wrapped packages, and a Christmas star are tucked into Dempsey's hands and arms, along with a wee sled and compact spruce tree. Darryl carries a mandolin, a golden cherub, and beaded garland in favorite Christmas colors. Both Santa figures wear thick fur caps and coats, brocade

An Old World Santa, Dietrich measures a full 38" and wears a coat and hat of vintage silk and velvet quilt. He has hand-carved wooden shoes from Holland. He holds lots of antique accessories including a bear, boat, tree, and other Christmas decorations and trimmings. $750.00.

Penrod is 30" tall and has glass eyes and a full, angora beard. He is a German Belsnickle Santa. He has snowshoes and is holding a large bag of toys. $400.00.

britches, and leather boots. Many of these accessories were found on Cheryl and Deanna's antiquing adventures.

"Deanna and I both love to travel together. When we go on the road, we always stop at every little town looking for old antique stores — and the more off-the-beaten-path, the better."

The Brenners' Santa dolls have polymer clay faces, hands, and feet. Bodies are constructed of wood and wire armatures with a hand-sewn body stocking fit over each form. The Santas typically have German glass eyes and bountiful beards (of which many are as white as the snow) made of Tibetan, Icelandic, and New Zealand wools. Costumes are made from vintage fabrics and wool pelts.

Cheryl designs her costume ensembles by eye, having learned how to sew at age 10 through the local 4-H program. Deanna was even younger; she learned to sew as an eight year old on her grandma's treadle sewing machine.

Deanna says she rarely uses patterns when cutting down old coats and sweaters. "Most of my patterns are ones that I have designed myself."

Each outfit is custom tailored, based on the type of Santa, the artist's research, and customer specifications. Accessory assemblages can include toys, jewelry, greenery, garland, bells, and other trinkets and baubles Cheryl and Deanna find on their frequent excursions to antique shops, flea markets, and garage sales, or that they buy from international outlets.

Noah V holds a menagerie of animals the two located at a specialty shop in Minnesota. Lucius wears a vintage silk gown in cream with an authentic priest's scarf over it. His cape is antique green velvet that is hand-beaded and embroidered. All wardrobe elements were unearthed at different antique shops: a vintage 1950s silk dress found in one was transformed into cassock and miter; an old Victorian table runner discovered in another became his cape. An antique brooch and a stamped metal band rimming the headdress, also found objects, complete the liturgical ensemble.

Cheryl says it is important that collectors know that "each one of their Santas is always special to us and every part is done

Noah V is a 30" Santa with mohair robe and brown leather shoes. He has a lush beard and holds tiny wooden animals in one hand and peace doves in the other. $485.00.

Lucius is a 30" St. Nicholas garbed in a gown of vintage silk with an authentic priest scarf. His cape is antique green velvet which is beaded and hand-embroidered. He has cream leather shoes and sculpted hands. $545.00.

with love. We sculpt and create each piece ourselves. That's why we love the fact that someone wants a part of us for their Christmas."

Besides Santa figures, Cheryl and Deanna make other types of dolls, including Samurai warriors, Geisha girls, mermaids, life-size baby dolls, and fashion and portrait dolls, but St. Nicholas in all his glorious manifestations remains their most beloved subject.

"He has such a wonderful history and there are so many different types. Most people just think of Santa as being the red and white Coca-Cola kind, so it's fun when a customer comes into our booth at a show and sees all the different types of Santas from around the world — especially when they see their own nationality represented."

Cheryl and Deanna have made Old World, traditional, Victorian, and as American as Fourth of July and Uncle Sam Santas. They have sculpted Santas from Germany, Poland, Italy, Norway, Scandinavia, Mexico, and one, Casimir, who suggested that he hail from Russia with his silver fox fur coat and cap and winter white beard. They have Santas ready to play golf or play hooky, and Santas gussied up for Mardi Gras or dressed down for bed. Cowboys, seamen, skiers, and mountain men, plus a Mr. posed with his Mrs. Claus, and still others, round out their holiday homage to the "right jolly old elf."

"We hope that people see the love and attention that has gone into each of our Santas," says Deanna. "They each take on a personality all their own."

Adds Cheryl: "I feel we really put every part of ourselves into our dolls. It doesn't matter if it is a small doll or a large one. Each Santa is special. Deanna and I both love Christmas so much and we know whoever ends up with one of our pieces loves Christmas as much as we do."

◆━◯━◆

Standing 36" tall, Casimir is elegant in silver fox fur coat and hat. He has antique velvet pants trimmed in fox, wooden shoes, and holds a slew of antique toys, a bottle brush tree wrapped in beaded glass garland, and lots of old Christmas decorations. $845.00.

Dempsey measures 32" tall and is outfitted in a magnificent dark green fur coat and stately hat and leather shoes. He carries an assortment of miniature toys and trims. $450.00.

Closeup of Dempsey.

Darryl is a 30" Father Christmas wearing a traditional blue English coat and hat of vintage fabric, along with richly brocaded pants. He wears beige leather boots and his hands are spilling over with Christmas accessories and finery. $450.00.

Flossie the Caroler is one of Lindy's Old Soul Friends, a limited edition series of 11" characters cast in resin. Each hand-painted character includes a certificate of authenticity with a description of the creation process. "Although Flossie lives a modest and frugal life, she is filled with joy and a saucy personality." $220.00.
Photo by Geoffrey Carr

From the Old Soul Santa resin series is Backwoods Santa, who follows the tradition of simple country folk, wearing a warm coat constructed of hand-me-down quilt fabric, and trimmed in fur collected from animals harvested for food. Standing 11" tall, he is a limited edition of 250 pieces that comes with a certificate of authenticity and a description of the creation process. $220.00.
Photo by Geoffrey Carr

11" Fishing Santa (Old Soul Santa series) clenches a pipe tightly between his teeth as he braves seasonal weather for the sport enjoyed by so many children and their parents. Smartly outfitted in a new slicker and boots, Fishing Santa has his reel ready for the catch and his brightly colored lures prepared. "The wriggling fish at the end of his pole demonstrates that his efforts are not without success." $220.00. Photo by Geoffrey Carr

12" paper clay and fabric Venetian Vanity draws its inspiration from sixteenth and seventeenth century Dutch paintings. Lindy loves making these Italian masque pieces that are intended to be hung on a wall. "These are different, for eclectic collectors who are looking for something special to hang." $150.00. Photo by Geoffrey Carr

## Mary Masters

Studio ....................Shipshewana, Indiana
E-mail ....................masterspc@aol.com
Website ..................www.marymasters.com
Medium..................Polymer clay
Dolls' Price Ranges..$65.00 – $10,000.00
Museums ...............Sauder Village in Archbold,
                      Ohio; the Kosciusko Jail
                      County Museum in Warsaw,
                      Indiana; and the Smithsonian
                      Institute in Washington, D.C.

## Wellspring:

"Faces. Many, many faces. Old, young, happy, sad. These inspire my creativity. Someone said to me once, 'You are going to run out of ideas.' I said, 'Not as long as there are faces.'

"I have a lot of ideas but not enough time to work on them. It used to bother me when people would say to me, 'You know what you should do?' Now I don't mind when they say that because I know that looking at my work has brought out the ideas they have, too. The imagination flows. The eyes of the school children get really big when they look at my work. The questions are many and they bring their parents to see me. Now these school children are bringing their children to see me. Those faces are my friends and my creative flow."

## Of Heritage and Headlines

Mary Masters recently sculpted a doll of one of the most beloved chiefs in the history of the Potawatomi Nation, of which she is a descendant. This autonomous and prosperous tribal unit originated in the Great Lakes area centuries ago and lived off the abundant natural resources of the area, trading with other tribes, and later, with the non-Indians, for whatever they could not catch in the lakes or hunt in the forests.

Mary tells the chief's story: "Pierre Moran was one of the last chiefs in Elkhart, Indiana. I heard he was tall and good-looking but deformed. I wanted to know why. So I went to the local museum and asked. No one there knew but they were nice enough to look in the stored papers in their basement.

"In the last filing cabinet we found a piece on Chief Moran in the June 27, 1906 issue of *The Elkhart Daily Review,* that was written by Edwin R. Beardsley, eldest son of Dr. Havilah Beardsley who, in 1831, surveyed and laid out Elkhart as a village. Although the story took place 75 years earlier when Edwin was just 18 years old, he remembered it with startling detail.

"It was the marrying time for Chief Benack's beautiful daughter, Maunee. Men came from all over to lay down their gifts to her. Maunee was to pick one man and she could make up her mind between two. These two men would have a hand-to-hand battle for her hand. Chief Pierre Moran won this battle.

"That night when Pierre went to bed in the wigwam, the other man came in the middle of the night and bit off his nose. Now Pierre had to kill this man so that he could marry the beautiful girl. The other man was a great tracker and had already gone from the village. Chief Pierre Moran got his knife and blanket and went after him.

"The next morning, Maunee went to the wigwam to wake up Pierre, but he was gone. There was nothing left except blood. So the people said, 'Pick another man. That one is dead.' Maunee said, 'No. I will wait.' She waited for one moon and then two moons. No Pierre. Finally, she had to pick another man.

"On the day of the wedding, Pierre came back and gave the scalp of the tracker to Maunee. Then Pierre and Maunee were married."

According to Mary, the man who shared the story of Chief Pierre Moran and his beautiful bride Maunee with young Edwin, Dr. Havilah Beardsley, knew that not having a nose greatly distressed Chief Moran, so he made one for him of wax. The Chief wore the wax nose in a sack around his neck and whenever he met someone new he would put it on.

"Dr. Beardsley and Chief Pierre Moran were friends for life. Because of this story I am here today. Pierre and Maunee were my great-great-great grandmother and grandfather."

## Creating "Masterpieces"

Chief Pierre Moran stands 14" to 15" tall on his oak base and with his fur headdress. He is the first of Mary's collectible originals with hands. In one he holds a knife; in the other, the scalp of the man who bit off his nose. $150.00.

Customers who visit Mary Masters' doll studio in picturesque Shipshewana, Indiana, have inquired so often if Native American Indians have a Santa Claus that the doll maker finally made one up.

A member of the Prairie Band of the Potawatomi Nation ("Keepers of the Fire"), Mary tells those who ask the same story: "If we had a Santa, he might have been from Europe. He would be wearing a Hudson Bay blanket, leather tunic and breeches, and the headdress of the Potawatomi with its beadwork and feathers."

In Mary's Native Christmas legend, there is a man who came and sang songs and made wooden animals to give to the children. He would arrive in the village on Christmas Eve, bearing his gifts and a Christmas tree, and would narrate the story of the birth of the Christ child.

"We call him Hairy-Face the Pioneer Santa."

Each year, the award-winning doll artist makes a Santa figure representative of a different country or culture, careful to keep the price under $100.00 so the dolls are accessible to all of her collectors. Each figure is patterned on a real person that Mary selects after deciding on the country whose traditions she will recall in her Santa sculpt.

Her most recent Santa, Hairy-Face the Pioneer Santa, is based on Mary's own saga of what might have been in the Potawatomi culture. He was made in the image of her husband, Robert DeWayne Masters.

Only one country is added to the Masterspiece Santa collection each year and each Santa figure has an oak base with a brass tag identifying the country he or she represents. Joulupukki or Yule Buck (Finland) is the latest Santa to join Mary's growing international family of 13" collectible Santa figures. $90.00.

⟡

"His eyes are the color of the sky and his cheeks are red from the cold air. Everyone likes Hairy-Face's open, smiling mouth and laughing, blue eyes."

Mary's growing Santa collection already includes gift givers from, among other countries, England, Scotland (Highlander Santa), Sweden (Santa Lucia or Queen of Lights), Norway, Italy, Poland, and Russia. She says that her red-haired Irish Santa is the most fun to make because of his pot of gold and leprechaun.

Once Mary has selected her latest country and model, she begins researching the yuletide stories.

"I have people from all over the world come in my store and I ask them, 'What is your Santa like?' When they get home, they send me the information and pictures. Plus, people are always asking me to 'do' their country."

For part of her research, Mary depends on grandmothers who visit her studio and those whom she meets on the Internet. She always invites them to share their Santa Claus traditions with her.

"Then I take the most told story and put it with the Santa. I make them so people will pass down their own heritage and not forget the stories of the elders."

Each year the oldest Santa in the collection is retired to make room for the new one. Already on the drawing board to follow up Hairy-Face is a Finnish Santa, known as Joulupukki (Yule Buck) in that country. Typical of her collectors, the Sneeringers of Ft. Wayne, Indiana, who bought Mary's Russian Grandfather Frost, shared some of Joulupukki's history with the sculptor:

"Popular radio programs from 1927 onwards probably had great influence in reformatting Finland's concept of Santa to resemble the American Santa Claus and to include reindeer and Korvatunturi (Mount Ear, near the Polar Circle) as their dwelling place, because there really are reindeer in Finland and they live up North.

"Korvatunturi is where Santa lives with his wife and a huge number of hardworking elves. Only elves can enter Santa's secret world inside at the North Pole, which is why no ordinary person has ever seen his workshop.

"Today, Finland is one of the few countries where children actually see Father Christmas in the act of delivering presents and probably the only country where he really does ask if they behaved during the year."

Mary enjoys watching visitors react to her various interpretations of Santa Claus, particularly those who spy a figure that is reflective of their own heritage. She fondly recalls the day an Italian woman entered her studio and spotted Mary's gray-haired La Befana replete with broomstick and an apron full of goodies.

"She was visiting America and could not speak English. She saw La Befana and left fast. I thought I did the Santa wrong. But no! She came back with her children and grandchildren. She said to them, 'Here is the real Santa.' It is the Santa from her childhood, the only Santa she knows."

Mary has been sculpting dolls since 1990, ever since her two young granddaughters, Mindy Eash and Sammira Little, both now grown, brought their grandmother a handful of clay from school and asked her to make them some dolls. The girls had been playing with Barbie® dolls but wanted some dolls that looked like them. Mary had no experience sculpting. She had never touched clay and had little faith in her ability to produce the desired dolls, but she discovered, to her granddaughter's delight and her surprise, that she was able to make two 9" dolls.

"Then they wanted the rest of the dolls' family. So I made them. To my surprise something wonderful was happening: 12" people began to appear all over the house. Some were made from people I had seen on television; some were made from pictures of people. All were made with love. But the best were made from memories or stories told by grandmothers."

Grandmothers are dear to Mary's heart. It was her own beloved grandmother (No-ko-mis) who inspired her Santa and Native American Indian collections, and the affordability of the dolls. Mary had been making fully articulated dolls that were priced out of range of many of her collectors. While she still makes these highly sought after one-of-a-kind dolls, many dressed in full regalia, the discovery of her grandmother's Skookum doll (Native American spirit doll) gave Mary a way to create original dolls and keep them priced under $100.00 each.

"Skookum dolls were made with wood bodies with a blanket wrapped around them. They had no hands and a clay face. The eyes go to the right to always help you have good health.

I can make the collection dolls faster because I only make the heads in clay, not the hands and feet, for the Native collection. I put hands on the Santas."

Mary makes a figure to add to her Santa and Native American Indian collectibles lines each year. All the dolls have heads sculpted of polymer clay. The bodies are made of wood, except for the arms, which are of copper wire for movement. Mary does all the sculpting as well as the bead and leather work herself. Her husband, a retired cabinetmaker, carves the dolls' bases from oak that Mary buys from the Amish community in Shipshewana, scraps that are left over from the church pews they make.

The Amish are also involved with hair for the dolls.

"The hair on my dolls is carded by the Amish ladies from different animal hair."

Mary compares each of her Santa creations to the birth of a new baby with her holding it, loving it, and molding it until it becomes the very best she can create.

"Then it happens. Someone else sees what I create and it makes a difference to them."

When visitors look at Mary's dolls, they tell the artist that they know each doll has a story to tell. Some of her customers drop by enough that they notice when a particular doll has been sold.

"One lady called and told me that she bought a doll of No-ko-mis, my grandmother. She put her on her nightstand so that every night she sees her smiling face and every morning she sees her smiling face and it makes her day because she has to smile, too.

"The people tell me every piece I do has a piece of my spirit in them. When a piece gets bought, people notice and miss them."

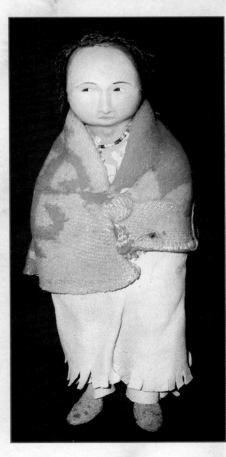

The Skookum doll that belonged to Mary's grandmother (No-ko-mis) is what gave the artist the ability to make affordable collectible dolls because of its simple design and construction.

In 1917 when the Communists seized power in Russia, religious celebrations were no longer tolerated. Christmas now became known as the festival of winter. The Christmas tree became the New Year tree and Santa Claus became Grandfather Frost. Dressed in a blue coat and carrying an armload of toys, Grandfather Frost helps families celebrate Christmas as in the days of Old Russia. $90.00.

With broom adorned with bell, La Befana, the Italian Gift Giver, is ready to fly. "She is one of the few women Santa figures in the world. She comes with a great story of how she became Santa." $90.00.

Representing Sweden is Santa Lucia with a crown of seven candles on her head and a tray laden with pastries in her hands. The candles help to light her way on her Christmas journey. Santa Lucia comes with a story card and a recipe to make the pastries. $90.00.

So accurate in its Biblical interpretation that it was awarded a certificate of authenticity, Mary's white gowned Jesus measures 13" tall. He holds a bowl to wash feet and a red belt scarf to wipe them. "The bowl is a copy of one bought in the land he was born by a nun so I can see the coloring and the way it was made. In the bowl is resin to look like water." $100.00.

## A Certificate of Historical Authenticity

This is to verify the Biblical accuracy and authentic likeness of the "It's a Masterpiece" sculpture of Christ Jesus. This rendition of Jesus takes into account the Biblical, historical, cultural, geographical, and genealogical aspects of Jesus of Nazareth. According to the book of Matthew, Jesus was a Hebrew of the lineage of Abraham, Isaac, Jacob, David, and Mary, all of whom were Jewish Israeli people. Because most traditional Biblical art is influenced by those well removed from the Middle Eastern region, the physical features of the Biblical Hebrew are usually misunderstood. It is my estimation that this replica of Jesus' person is very much authentic to His true likeness.

Rev. Gary A. Hoffman
Master of Arts Middle Eastern History
Clear Lake Baptist Church, Fremont, Indiana

13" Irish Santa is "the most fun." He has a derby hat with a four leaf clover on it, blue and green plaid cloak, and yellow vest. Available with either red or white beard, Irish Santa is trimmed with a pot of gold and, hidden in the tree he holds, a leprechaun to watch over his gifts. $90.00.

# Needle Arts

Mother and Child by Sherry Goshon. This commissioned vignette features sculpted faces which have cloth applied over them. Mother is 20" and Child is 5", and each has a body of cloth. Both figures are dressed in hand-dyed silks and the baby has a blanket made from an antique handkerchief. $1,200.00. Photo by Sherry Goshon

## Dru Esslinger

Studio ....................Madison, Kansas
E-mail ....................drue@madtel.net
Website ..................www.drusilla.com
Medium..................Cloth
Dolls' Price Ranges..$50.00 – $350.00
Member..................Pin Ella P's

## Wellspring:

"People provide me with a continuous flow of ideas that I can use for creating more dolls."

## Behind the Scenes

*The Art of the Doll Maker* is a 1999 movie about healing through the arts. Lee Hubbard Crowe, who conceived the film, hopes the movie will help women feel they are not isolated in dealing with a personal loss.

The film narrates the experiences of Dru Esslinger's family in dealing with the loss of her daughter. Featured in the movie, directed by Mel Metcalfe III, are Dru, Lisa Lichtenfels, elinor peace bailey, E.J. Taylor, and other doll artists. A recipient of four awards for documentary filmmaking, it is available in VHS and DVD formats and can be ordered by calling (888) 880-8365.

## Stitch Sculpting

Dolls entered Dru Esslinger's life just before her beloved 28-year-old daughter, Mary Katherine Esslinger Haworth, known simply as Kathy, departed it. Several months prior to Kathy's death of ovarian cancer in 1985, the two women had discovered the playful doll patterns of renowned fiber artist elinor peace bailey. For a brief time, mother and daughter worked side-by-side making dolls, Kathy in her hospital bed embroidering faces and Dru in a nearby chair making cloth bodies.

Making dolls filled Dru's time between Kathy's many operations and recuperations. She started out slowly, stitching up a doll here and there, pouring her love into the dolls, nurturing and coddling them, as she dealt with her daughter's declining health and eventual death. Dru fell easily into her stitching rhythm, inspired by a lifetime of influences and experiences in creating her soft sculptures.

Born and raised in the Flint Hills of Kansas, Dru attended a one-room school and took part in cattle drives as a child. During the next 30 years, she attended college, became a farmer's wife, taught elementary school, raised four children, and became involved in church and 4-H work.

Sherry says that her 20" Oceanna figure "just happened." She had bought an Oriental fabric in New Mexico and found a greeting card featuring a tattooed mermaid in a shop, and the combined results were Oceanna. Sherry was so intent on beginning Oceanna that she set to work immediately and nearly finished the doll while still in New Mexico. $1,200.00.

Chantal was modeled after one of Sherry's favorite designers, Erte (Russian-born painter Romain de Tirtoff who was one of the foremost fashion designers of the early twentieth century). "That whole Art Deco time period just excites me." The 22" doll wears all silks and her dog (out of camera range,) is a Nancy Garwon design. $1,100.00.

Caitlin-Keeper of Children's Books is the first in a series of six fairies in a rainbow of colors, including blue, green, pink, and cream. The 16" doll is named for the granddaughter of an Australian friend who loves fairies and books. Caitlin is wearing all hand-dyed silks. "I love dying fabrics and silks are so yummy!" $800.00.

Nicholas, a 22" felt doll, was inspired by a greeting card that featured a little boy angel. "I e-mailed my friend Nancy Garwon, who does animals for me, and I only had the little boy's head finished. I said, 'This little boy angel wants a dog,' and in a few days, Nancy sent pictures." Together, Nicholas and his dog, Daisey, are a match made in heaven. $1,300.00.

Beige stands 25" tall and is painted cloth. She looks adorable in her vintage toddler baby cotton crocheted dress slipped over a 1930s reproduction fabric dress and pants ensemble that Sue made. Beige hugs her favorite kitty cat doll, dressed in red checks with white apron. $275.00.

Margaret-Ann's hair is designed of black paint textured with a medium brush stroke. Her body is of tea-dyed muslin. She wears a dress of blue and white checked homespun, along with tea-dyed muslin bloomers and slip, and all of her wardrobe pieces are trimmed with antique lace. She wears a removable bonnet of matching homespun.

"I love the old folk art dolls and the dolls pioneer women made for their children, the well-loved penned and painted cloth dolls of those days. I try to capture that simple, sweet look of a child's face, and to make someone really want to hold one of my dolls and feel attached to it the way I know these children must have been attached to their homemade dolls."

Three years ago, the doll maker broadened her range to include black dolls. Her mission remains the same: to create beautiful dolls that allow her to combine her talents to achieve an endearing, elegant simplicity.

Coppery Kacinda achieves her high-cheeked good looks from Sue's method of tacking down small bits of cotton balls, one for each cheek and one each for nose and chin areas, over which cotton fabric is stretched and tacked in the back of the doll's head.

"This gives more dimension to the doll's face. I don't do this a lot, but it is interesting to get a rounded cheek look."

Pretty Beige has richly burnished skin and luminous eyes, along with a head full of light-tipped natural wool hair. She wears a 1930s print collared blouse and elastic-waist pants beneath a vintage crocheted dress. She holds a handmade embroidered 1920s-style black cloth cat.

"The beauty and depth that can be achieved with African-American skin tones is such a challenge and such a joy for me. Each face will turn out differently and the glow of the skin tone from a light mocha skin coloring to a deep dark skin coloring is the range I just love working with.

"Painting these skin tones is always a learning experience. That is what I enjoy the most, the trial and error and the discovery of a new technique of overlaying colors and getting the look I want."

Color is a crucial element in Sue's work. She admits that her efforts to match the vision in her mind's eye on her dolls sometimes borders on obsession as she combines and layers colors hours upon end to achieve the desired results.

"Color in paint and fabric is almost always the total inspiration for every doll I make. I might come across a color combination or pattern just by taking a walk outside in the garden or seeing a colorful outfit someone is wearing."

With her painted cloth doll named Carrie-Ann, Sue found inspiration in the color and pattern of a 1920s-style yellow fabric that features little dolls dressed in blue and pink party frocks and pinafores.

"This is a darling print that sat for a couple weeks until I came across a vintage baby sweater with tiny buttons that had just the right coloring. The whole doll came to me then."

What Sue envisioned was a 27" cloth doll with violet eyes, pert nose, and tousled auburn hair and wearing a dress with Peter Pan collar beneath a knit sweater over lace-edged bloomers and a petticoat slip. A violet ribbon adorns her crown and pink fabric shoes with ribbon ties cover her feet. Carrie-Ann clutches a pancake-style doll that looks strikingly similar to the dolls on her dress right down to the smooth cap of hair and A-line dress.

Another doll inspired by color and fabric is October, a dark-skinned beauty that took its design cues from the pastels of the Easter season.

"I had a combination of Easter colors come to me at a time when I was obsessed with the idea of using lavender and pale yellow on a black doll. So I hand-dyed some cotton gauze and some flannel and worked with that until I came up with an outfit that was in my mind's eye.

"I was so obsessed with getting my idea out into a doll that October just came together in a day and a half."

Sometimes Sue's dolls — or her children, as she likes to think of them — will detour from her original concept or sketch so she is careful to let the doll tell her "what she wants to look like." Other times, Sue will encourage design detours in order to get out of a creative slump.

"To spur my imagination I'll sometimes make up one of my basic doll bodies and then rely on the painting and the hair to make it unique. Since I didn't work with patterns before I started making dolls, I don't have a fear of sticking to any guidelines; I just manipulate whatever medium I'm using without worrying about whether or not I'm doing it the correct way.

"I'm a very hands-on artist and I'll do whatever I need to do in order to get the right look for my dolls."

⊰⊷◉⊶⊱

Although inspired by Easter, the 22" doll with sun-tipped wool hair and wrapped in a gauzy confection of lavender and yellow is named October. She came together exactly as her designer envisioned her, right down to her jacket with embroidered flourish and accessories that include a vintage button necklace and twisty hair tie, also of gauze. (She sold within a day.) $275.00.

Brianna-Marie was built around the red curls of hand-dyed Tibetan lamb's wool amassed on her crown. The 24" doll is given an old-world look with her hand-appliquéd wool tabard. $295.00.

Sue's 15" Carrie-Ann was inspired by a piece of fabric and a vintage baby sweater. "She just came together from those items." She is painted cloth with stitch-sculpted nose and woven back mohair for wig. Vintage baby shoes and sweater complete her ensemble. $285.00.

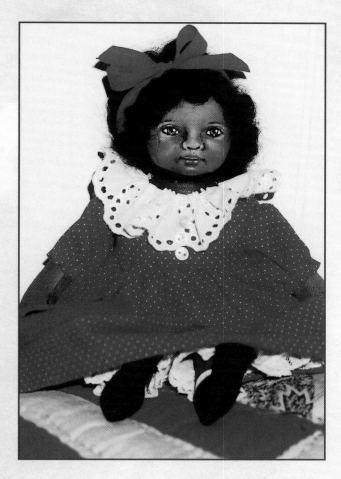

Patience derived her name from the very virtue for which she is named. She was Sue's personal (and time-consuming) challenge to see just how small she could make a rounded-head, sculpted-nose doll that still retained a strong childlike presence. Standing a petite 9", Patience, with wavy wool crepe hair, wears a dress of red polka-dots with vintage lace collar and lace-trimmed bloomers, as well as painted socks and shoes. $190.00.

Sue enjoys painting gourds in wildlife and Native American Indian themes. $885.00.

# *Wellspring*

*"With the babies, I go through this process where I see them go through nine months of development in my hands, just like real babies, but over the course of so many weeks. It is a birth and a new baby is born."*

-Lorna Miller-Sands

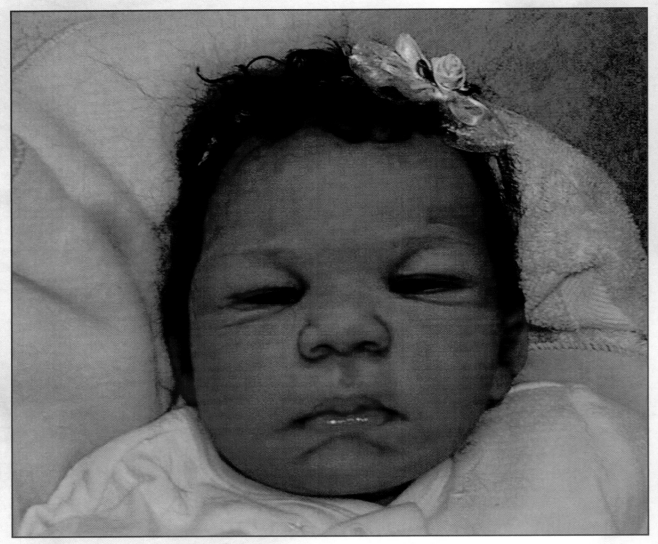

Jaelin by Lorna Miller-Sands. Sweet little Jaelin is a 22" biracial baby girl with enormous green eyes who is just about to go down for her afternoon nap. "I wanted to do a squinty-eyed baby that looked like a newborn and Jaelin was born." $2,300.00.
Photo by Lorna Miller-Sands

## Cheri Hiers

Home/Studio ..........Ormond Beach, Florida
E-mail ....................Ladd123@aol.com or
                            cherihiers@hotmail.com
Website ..................www.theartistdoll.com/cherihiers.html
Media .....................Polymer clay and porcelain
Dolls' Price Ranges ..$325.00+

## Wellspring:

"Sometimes while visiting antique fairs or shops, I'll see an old inkwell or other vessel and I can picture a little fairy sitting on it. Sometimes I picture the exact colors they will have.

"I love creating the cup and saucer fairy; they are still my number one calling, but the most fun is creating a fairy on other, more usual finds — this is where I sometimes have to visualize just what position would be best for the overall finished piece — and sensing the inspiration is coming from my heart."

## Winging It

The wings Cheri Hiers uses for her little fairies are real butterfly wings that she purchases from dealers from around the world.

"These butterflies, reared in butterfly houses, live a full happy life and when they pass they are preserved and sold to collectors.

"I thank each butterfly for the wings they leave behind, as they move into their next life."

By giving the butterfly wings new purpose as fairy wings, the artist feels she is extending the beauty of these fragile and magnificent little creatures for generations to come. She identifies her fairies by the butterfly wings they are wearings and each figurine is as unique in personality, style, and spirit as individual people.

The butterfly wings are an essential element in the artist's work and philosophy for she believes that butterflies and fairies live together and live the same dream.

"Butterflies dream of being fairies and fairies wish they were butterflies. Butterflies are a little more daring and come out more often to visit the world the rest of us live in!"

## In the Blink of an Eye

Cheri Hiers isn't exactly sure what her sprightly little fairies do when she's not looking, but she knows they are having a good time. Reading, giggling, playing — these are the same gleeful pursuits she suspected her teddy bears of enjoying after lights out when she was a child struggling to stay awake in her bed and catch them at their merriment.

"I had so many stuffed toys that my mother built shelves in my bedroom for all my teddy bears. I just knew they would come down from those shelves and play all night long while I was asleep. I never was able to stay awake and I never did catch them!"

Today, Cheri ascribes the same magical quality to her delicate one-of-a-kind porcelain and polymer clay fairies that she once attributed to her beloved teddy bear playmates.

"To me, fairies are special little beings who truly love nature and all it has to offer. They enjoy a world of complete bliss, where happiness abounds and every single day brings a new reason to rejoice."

Ten years ago when she spied a dainty elfin doll named Willow made by original doll and doll mold artist Dianna Effner, Cheri sensed she had found her bliss.

"I knew right away that this was the road I wanted to go down, that of the whimsical world of little fairies."

She knew nothing about dolls or sculpting (although she sensed sculpting would be like drawing, only in 3-D), but was determined to create her own fine art figurines. Inspired by Effner, Cheri envisioned an array of pixies with come-hither eyes, brilliant butterfly wings, and perhaps an iridescent sprinkling of fairy dust that would appeal to collectors in much the same way as a piece made by artist John Wright had caught her eye and mesmerized her with its charm and craftsmanship.

"My first glimpse at Diane Effner's Willow is what opened my eyes to doll making. Seeing one of John Wright's pieces, a little pixie sitting on a tomato red pin cushion, is what led me to become a doll maker."

The self-taught artist now has her own line of lilliputian-size figurines called Lauren Alexander Teacup Fairies, named after her son and daughter. She credits her multi-talented mother for her own natural creativity and spent years developing and refining her skills by watching sculpting videos and remaining immersed in the process of making dolls. One of her trademark touches in her doll making is the use of real butterfly wings, imported from around the world. She has also developed an application to give her dolls' inset eyes the shine and realism of glass eyes.

The fairies are not given names, but are referred to by the wings they wear. Because they are all one-of-a-kind creations, just like little people, each has a perceptibly unique personality. Cheri includes a signed hang-tag with each fairy that bears a title number for identification.

Cheri haunts local antique shops and fairs in search of props and pieces she can integrate into her miniature tableaux. She discovers fabrics and accessories like lace and crystal, acorns, and flora everywhere she looks. Mohair, lamb's wool, human hair, and lately viscose are the artist's picks for her fairies' crowning glory. The delicate faces boast hand-applied eyelashes, sun-blushed cheeks, and softly sweet expressions that seem to simply emerge beneath Cheri's sculpting tools.

"I just feel what my heart wants to create."

Each fairy is designed as part of a vignette and tucked into the dwelling that most perfectly suits her: an antique teacup, a trinket box, stemware,

◆⟹⟸◆

Morpha Catanarius is one of the artist's earlier pieces. Just 4½" tall by 5½" wide, she has enormous, blue eyes and milky white Tibetan lamb's hair and wears wee flocked slippers. $375.00.

hand-painted plates, a tiny bench — even a cozy wooden, porcelain or glass shoe.

"I find things that look like a fairy should be part of it. I find many vessels in antique shops, as well as new pieces that might attract a fairy to visit."

Morpho Catanarius sits on a hand-painted porcelain candleholder, contemplating the secret world inside the prism she dangles. With garland wreath upon her head and tiny elfin booties snuggling her feet, as well as exotic white wings tipped in black, she is enchanting from head to toe. Attacus Atlas roosts on a trinket box that appealed to Cheri because it looks like an antique. With pert, pursed lips as well as glorious multi-hued wings and long, blonde braided hair, Attacus Atlas seems to know how endearing she is.

Cheri's work is characterized by an ebullient energy caught in the cherubic visages and dynamic vignettes of her fairies. A fairy named Pompona Intermedia perches prettily on a old-fashioned sewing machine that Cheri found on one of her many foraging expeditions for striking vessels. The tiny figure wears jewel-encrusted wings and a rakish paper hat.

"For some reason that little paper hat just seemed to work on this piece. The fairies tell me what works — especially when it comes to the wings."

Tosena Splendida and Acticus Dubernardi are The Lamplighters on their well-turned antique candlestick and vintage oil lamp — the kind that was lit with whale oil in the days of yore. Wearing caps fitted around their little elfin ears and sweet smiles, these fairies' wings narrate the beauty of

❖⇐══◎══⇒❖

Sporting a turban-like topknot made from a strip of handkerchief for her headpiece, Attacus Atlas stands approximately 9½" tall by 9" wide. She has a mohair wig and inset eyes. $375.00.

Pompona Intermedia is the sewing fairy. She has Tibetan lamb's hair and inset eyes. Her wings are sparked with hand-applied rubies, emeralds, and blue and pink sapphires. $375.00.

Cheri says that her fairy, Cithaerium Aurorina, has one of the sweetest temperaments of any she has made to date. With a crown of lustrous viscose hair and wide-open and penetrating eyes, this fairy looks as though she knows all the secrets of the world. In private collection.

the butterflies from which they came. Others are busy sharing secrets and watching the world go by and being thoroughly charmed by it.

"Fairies live in a world that can be shared with both young and old. It just takes a little imagination to head down a path of enchantment."

That path of enchantment is well-worn by Cheri who frequents it in her quest to capture the ethereal and mystical essence of fairies and render it in her porcelain and clay creations. One lesson she has learned in her years of sculpting fairies: she must keep still and listen to what her fairies say as she sculpts.

"Sometimes they say, 'No, I don't want that color hair or those particular wings.' Sometimes they say, 'I want blue eyes, not the green you were planning on.' Sometimes they just say, 'Thanks for bringing me here!'"

That was the case with the sweet-natured Cithaerium Aurorina, whose gratitude can be seen in her shining brown eyes. A favorite piece of the artist's because of her bashfulness, this fairy is dressed demurely in a bit of antique lace accented by a ruby choker. Her glossy mane of hair, held back with a flower-sprigged band, is made of viscose.

"Viscose is very thin, like angel hair. It is wonderful stuff to work with and it's probably been used for a hundred years — but I just discovered it six months ago!"

After working on small-scale fairies for nearly 10 years, the artist feels ready to pursue her heart's desire of sculpting larger pieces.

"When I look at my first fairies, I see already how they are getting larger and larger. I even had a dealer call with a special order a few weeks back. She had a customer who collects my work request that I make her a smaller piece — like my older pieces. It's funny but before she called to ask this, I didn't really realize how my gals were getting a little bigger.

One of her first ones, Stichophthalma Camedeva, measures just 5½" tall and, although sold, remains a cherished figure. The fairy sits upon an upside-down hand-painted teacup and wears a beaded snood. She is one that the artist plans to revisit at some point in the future.

"I know I will always create my little fairies, but I want to move onto young adult fairies, more flowing, maybe some of these little ones as they grow up in a few years!"

Regardless of size, Cheri's little brood of sprites will remain true to fairy form: "Tradition has it that fairies can be seen only between one blink of the eye and the next."

So while the doll maker may never catch her fairies at their fun, she believes in their magic and knows in her heart that they are living the good life.

Tosena Splendida sits upon a candlestick and Acticus Dubernardi perches on an antique oil lamp, both lighting the way in this charming vignette. $375.00 each.

Stichophthalma Camedeva is picture-pretty at 5½" tall by 5½" wide on her Bohemian glass teacup that is hand-painted with a raised floral motif. $375.00.

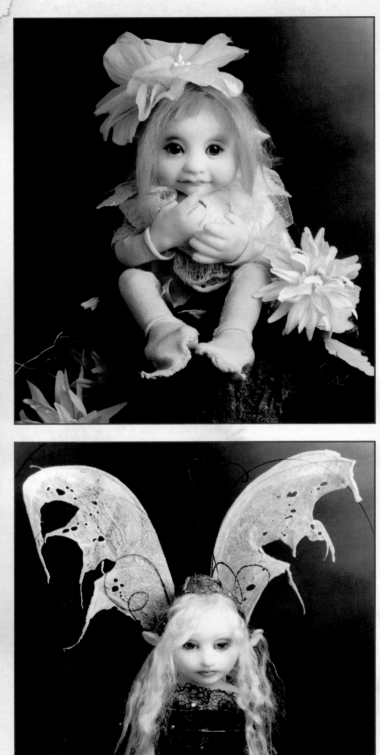

dolls' faces, like Gail's spirited pierrots, are painted and all of the costumes are hand-stitched and trimmed.

"Some of my loves are antique fabrics, beads, and baubles, which I incorporate into all my pieces. I dye and distress newer fabrics to give them a gentle, lived-in look.

"I like to use found objects in my work also to add a bit of the unexpected."

Little Elf Girl radiates personality with her enormous, wide-open blue glass eyes and sweetly upturned mouth. At a petite 8", this woodland will-o'-the-wisp has a mop of red hair punctuated with a floppy white flower. Gail calls her satyr, Romulus, a "sweet goat guy" that she pictures seeking his heart's true love in the forest.

"I can see him clumping around the woods, peeking around trees looking for Mrs. Romulus."

The dashing, debonair Master Hedgehog sports new and antique fabrics that Gail dyed and distressed and fashioned into shirt and vest. Trimmed with striped scarf and lounging slippers, this lovable phantasm is 9" tall and has an acorn carry-all.

"I like to do things that make viewers laugh and think a bit. I always picture my weird little men as funny, but I see my fairies differently. They are mostly mysterious and untouchable but not unapproachable. A good art piece draws you in or evokes an emotion."

Oona, an ethereal being based on a character in Ridley Scott's 1985 fantasy adventure movie, *Legend,* is hauntingly beautiful with vivid but hooded blue eyes, fragile wings, and a slip of a dress ornamented with black .metallic lace overlay. To Gail, her look seems to suggest introspection, a contemplation of the origins of the universe.

"When I look at Oona, I always wonder what she's thinking. I'm usually ready to let a piece go once I'm done with it, but I kept Oona. I just couldn't let her go."

⊰⊱⊷⊶⊰⊱

Little Elf Girl is polymer clay over wire armature. She stands just 8" tall and has a mop of red mohair. In private collection.

Polymer clay Oona is dressed in antique metallic fabrics. Seated, she is about 11", including wings. Not for sale. Photos by Gail Lackey

Madame and The Marquis is a painted, polymer clay vignette over wire armatures. The dolls are 26" tall and wear costumes of vintage fabrics. "I like to think of them as decadent in a seventeenth century French ballroom!" Each piece sold for $3,000.00.
Photo by Welsh Studios

⋆⟞◉⟞⋆

Gail creates subjects and themes based on the prevailing dictates of her mood. She admits she gets bored very easily and, like a fairy flitting from blossom to bloom, she will bounce from one topic to another, propelled purely by impulse. She has made mermaids, fairies, elves, moon men, novelty pieces, and her so-called cast of weird but beloved little men.

"The only things I haven't done are realistic children!"

When whim and whimsy strikes, she has to act on it immediately or risk losing her creative flow. Master Hedgehog was the result of one such compulsion that surfaced unexpectedly and persisted until she had fully sculpted the piece. Other dolls come about because she is called to certain historic eras, a favorite being seventeenth century France. Madame and The Marquis, a pair of French aristocrats dressed to the Baroquian nines in their silk and beaded finery, were made after one such imaginary sojourn.

"I adore the costumes of this period and I have tons of books showing all the different fashions. I love the big, high hairdos and the beauty marks. Making Madame and The Marquis was something I'd always wanted to do. They were big dolls for me. Most of my pieces are 8" to 10" tall; these dolls, including their hair, are 26" tall."

Pierrot Serenading the Moon was inspired by Gail's fascination with the automatons, the little mechanical figures on velvet bases, of the 1800s. Outfitted in antique fabrics from head to toe, the pierrot wears silk velvet pants studded with gold metal sequins and a gold jacket of vintage brocade and trimmed with silver bullion. He holds a violin while reclining on a celluclay moon that stares at him with large glass eyes, lips pursed and brow furrowed.

A lifelong lover of children's picture books who once penned her own story about a silly elf girl in a forest, Gail wants her figures to appear as though they just stepped out of whatever fairy tale or fable in which they might belong, dressed for the part and ready to spin out their stories in a three-dimensional realm.

Scary Story epitomizes Gail's goal through a favorite character of hers: a little, old grandma elf. The vignette features one such elf, wizened but wise and sitting on an old wooden spool with her wide-eyed grandbaby, outfitted adorably in its tiny acorn hat.

"It looks to me like Grandma is telling the baby not to go into the forest because there are big trolls there. The grandbaby is wringing her hands and saying, 'Ohhhhh.'"

Recently, Gail stepped into the fourth dimension with the creation of Marley's Ghost, a cobweb-covered shade in clothing from the 1800s and hand-painted glass eyes. Every now and then she will sculpt a boudoir doll – a "bed doll" that reclines on a chaise or bed and that was all the rage of the rip Roaring Twenties. They were typically garbed in snazzy pantsuit ensembles to symbolize the new rebellious woman and were made not for children but for adults. Many movie stars of the day toted them about as one might a pocketbook or a muff.

"The heads of the dolls were usually composition and the bodies were cloth with very elongated limbs. The most popular boudoir dolls were very vampish-looking with lots of smoky eyeshadow and the 'smokers.' These were the same size as the full-size boudoir dolls, only with holes in their mouths where wooden dowels, painted like cigarettes, were inserted to look as if the dolls were actually smoking."

Using her boudoir dolls as models, Gail also sculpts an occasional tassel doll. These legless pieces with fringed skirts consist of head, torso, and arms and hang from cords in the tops of their heads. Lately, she has been toying with the idea of sculpting miniature dolls that will explore the same fantasy themes as her larger pieces: elves, fairies, and fairytale people.

"Hopefully my work brings a smile to the viewer and transports them, if only for a moment, to a magical place in time, to a land of wonder and enchantment!"

Gail's Scary Story vignette depicts a grandma elf and her grandbaby, sculpted of polymer clay over wire armatures. The figures have hand-painted faces. Their clothing is made of gauzes dyed and distressed and the baby wears a little acorn cap. Both are seated on an old antique spool. In private collection.
Photo by Gail Lackey

❖══◑═◐══❖

❖══◑═◐══❖

Master Hedgehog is polymer clay over wire armature. He wears antique and new fabrics dyed and distressed. 9" tall. In private collection.
Photo by Gail Lackey

Romulus is a 16" polymer clay sculpt satyr that Gail hand painted. The fur on his legs is Norwegian sheep. In private collection.
Photo by Smith Studios

The 18" Pierrot Serenading the Moon is constructed of hand-painted polymer clay over wire armature. The Pierrot wears antique fabrics and the moon is sculpted of celluclay and has blue glass eyes. $1,995.00.
Photo by Gail Lackey

## Lorna Miller-Sands

Studio ....................Mt. Joliet, Tennessee
E-mail .....................lornam123@aol.com
Website ..................www.lornamiller-sands.com
Medium...................Polymer clay
Dolls' Price Ranges ..$2,395.00 – $4,500.00
Member..................Artists United

## Wellspring:

"My children, particularly my baby girl, Baylee, inspire me. I couldn't have been blessed with a more perfect model."

## Baby Factory

In 2003, Lorna Miller-Sands introduced three limited edition (35 pieces each) realistic black babies: Julora, Nikkea, and Kiaree. Made of resin, the babies are 16" newborns with fully articulated arms and legs and posable, weighted bodies. Hair is mohair, accented with hat, bow, or headband, and eyes are painted. The infants are dressed in diapers and t-shirts and come with toys and blankets. A white resin baby makes her debut next. Available through several dealers (links are available through Lorna's website), the babies are priced at $895.00 each.

Lorna recently inked a deal with Ashton-Drake Galleries to sculpt four 22", open edition babies that will retail in the neighborhood of $150.00 to $160.00 each. The first piece will be a black baby, followed by a biracial baby and then two others. "These babies will be made of a vinyl silicone material that will give them an extremely realistic look and feel."

## Labor of Love

"I'm in labor without the pain!"
This is how realistic baby doll artist Lorna Miller-Sands gleefully describes her occupation.

"The fact that I am a mother of four children creating these life-like babies makes my job the best in the world."

And make no mistake, these babies, conceived in Lorna's very fertile imagination and constructed of a blend of Super Sculpey™ and Fimo™, are lifelike — so much so that their "mother" is regularly besieged by well-meaning folks who want to cuddle and coo at the little darlings.

"When I walk around with one of these little creatures, people cannot tell they are dolls. I had one of the babies with me in church once and I got lots of stares and smiles. One time, I had two of the babies in a hotel bar and I got plenty of mean looks until people figured out they weren't real.

"It's only when people touch the dolls that they realize they are not real babies."

Having four real-life models underfoot, including a new baby daughter, helps Lorna achieve her trademark verisimilitude in the visages of the babies, a quality particularly evident in their richly nuanced skin tones. Another authenticating touch is the artist's use of her own children's downy, soft hair on the heads of her clay babies.

"I harvest hair about every three months. Then I snip pieces of it for the babies, embed it in the clay, and bake the heads."

Each of Lorna's babies, some newborns, some infants of several months, weighs in at six to eight pounds and measures between 19" and 22" long. They are fitted with glass eyes and posable heads and garbed in infant clothing bought off the rack. Just like any proud new mama, Lorna is picky about clothing choices, selecting soft and sweet ensembles that she completes with stuffed animals, fleece blankets, and identification bracelets.

Each tiny gold bracelet bears the name that Lorna has painstakingly contrived for the doll, arranging letters together to form interesting appellations as she runs down the alphabet: Ajani, Collette, Jarren, Niasha. On average, she creates three babies a month, devoting up to 14 hours a day to each doll over a two-week gestation period.

"When I start a baby, I have a basic idea of what I want to do. I kind of let the clay take me where it wants. The baby that starts out with a wide-open mouth may want it closed. I'm often surprised by the end results.

"I am a very emotional, very passionate person and this is very visible in the faces of my creations. The dolls are definitely extensions of me and I have been told that I am just like my dolls."

Alicia, with her wide-open eyes and gently parted lips, is one of Lorna's babies that reflects not only the depth of expressiveness of the artist but the seemingly independent will of the baby to manifest its own identity.

Lorna began sculpting dolls in the early 1990s, focusing exclusively on toddler girls for the first nine years of her doll making career. She had come to the United States from Nassau, Bahamas, a decade earlier to study art at a private school in California. After earning her degree

Alicia is a 23" white baby. "I wanted to do a real chubby, wide-eyed baby." Alicia has blue eyes and mohair covered in a baby cap. $2,395.00.

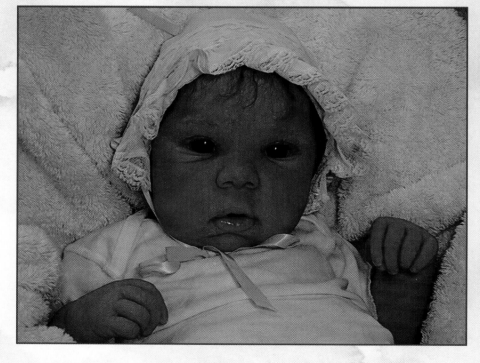

145

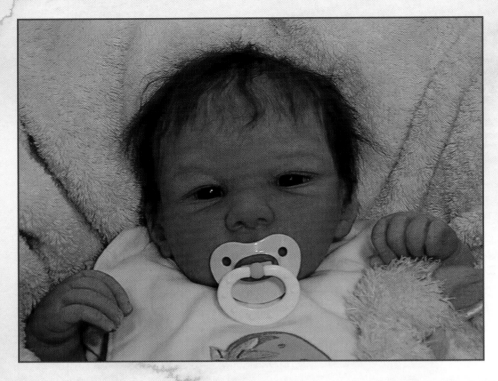

Kimberlyn is one of the artist's first white babies. "Hers was a face that was inspired by a photo that I saw." $2,395.00.

in drawing, Lorna worked as a telemarketer until a vacation in Germany revealed her true heart's desire.

"My friend and I were walking around in Hamburg and I saw these very contemporary, realistic dolls in a shop. I knew at that moment that I was destined to be a sculptor."

By the end of the 1990s, Lorna's biological clock began ticking; she knew she wanted to make babies — and the notion was only reinforced at a trade show where she was exhibiting her toddler dolls. There were life-size babies everywhere, beautifully rendered in polymer clay and dressed to the nines in their smartly accessorized infantwear. Lorna was immediately hooked.

"I knew at that moment that creating realistic baby dolls was what I was supposed to be doing. Once I started making these babies, I realized why I was put on this planet."

Although artistic by nature and education, Lorna considers herself a self-taught sculptor. Her influences have come from her children and not from any other artists, although she credits realistic baby artist Eva Helland with inspiring her to create the ultimate baby doll.

Collectors have told her that her babies have heart and soul. Collections of her dolls can be seen in doll shops in the United States and in the United Kingdom.

The recipient of numerous awards, Lorna is one of the very few black doll artists making realistic black babies on the contemporary doll scene. She has earned worldwide recognition for her black babies and can barely keep up with demand. She has garnered accolades for her realistic work from her peers, premier realistic baby doll artist Eva Helland among them, for its originality and diligent attention to detail.

Recently, the naturalized United States citizen has added a new bundle of newborns to her Tennessee nursery/studio: Caucasian babies. Baby Kimberlyn was one of the first white arrivals; Lorna felt the baby exceeded her expectations when she first started work on her from a photograph she saw and admired.

"I was challenged by the idea put to me by a collector of sculpting a white baby. I feel that as a black baby artist I am capable of doing different nationalities, but I didn't have all the confidence in the beginning with the white babies that I had with my black babies. Now the confidence is there and people are buying them hand over fist."

With both black and white babies under her belt, so to speak, Lorna decided to tackle another doll making frontier: a biracial baby, a beautiful blending of black and white skin tones and features that are at once subtle and distinctive.

"Nobody else was doing biracial babies or, if they were, they weren't necessarily doing the black and white mixed race babies. I thought, 'Why not?' I love a challenge and it gives me diversity."

Creating biracial babies, like beautiful chubby-cheeked and green-eyed Jaelin, also gives the artist another opportunity to showcase her signature "top secret formula" for capturing different skin tones, particularly what she says is the the real skin tone of black people that is evident in baby Shawnee. It is this particular attribute that Lorna believes sets her work apart from other artists making black babies.

"When it comes to my black babies, I know I give my collectors something no one can because I am able to capture the real essence of a black baby and that is the subtle skin tones. That's an edge I have on the competition — that and having my own babies and seeing them up close and in person."

Babies like Nikeema, Nicholas, and Shawnee show the range of color and tones Lorna is able to effectuate with her paints and brushes. Nikeema and Nicholas are both light-skinned black babies with Nicholas being just a whisper of a shade darker. Shawnee is a newborn whose skin hasn't quite reached the depth and evenness of pigment it will ultimately achieve.

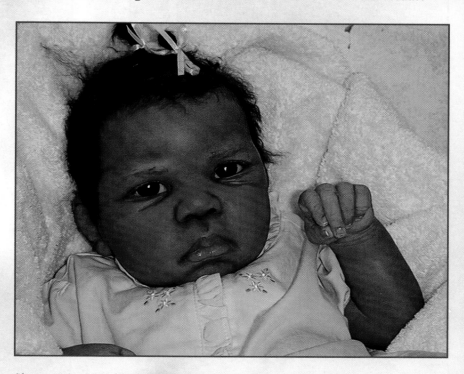

"Being a mother, there's just something fascinating about giving birth, about creating these little babies in all their beautiful colors. It's a birthing process. It's a really wonderful feeling, knowing you're creating these babies and knowing the happiness that the babies give. The people who collect them love these little babies. That makes it really fulfilling for me."

Lorna's doll artistry articulates what she values most about being a mother — a fitting testimonial for the artist who found herself and her purpose in making babies.

Shawnee is a 22" black baby. "With Shawnee, I really wanted to capture skin tone. When black babies are first born, especially dark-skinned babies, there are real obvious tone differences and I wanted to show the gradation of color in her hands. It's like her hands haven't really found their pigment yet." $2,395.00.

"The Evolving Artist" is a fitting title for this final chapter. The book will come to a close but the story of each artist carries on with each piece of art created. It is a series of new beginnings, each piece its own story, yet part of the life narrative of the artist.

These are the latest works of the artists about whom you've just read. It is where their next chapters begin.

## Jean Bernard
Pamela's Journey features a mermaid on a snail, a commissioned piece sculpted of Aves Apoxie Sculpt and polymer clays. It was made in honor of Jean's dear friend and her journey with Multiple Sclerosis. "This girl should not have anything but pleasure in her life. She is the ultimate gift from heaven." The sculpt took Jean six months to complete and now resides in her friend's home. Not for sale.
Photo by Jean Bernard

## Jean Bernard
Twelve Dreamers is an "emotional dance" wrought in a silver chair that allowed Jean to convey herself through her art. Made of Aves Apoxie Sculpt and acrylic paints, it calls to mind a Dream Catcher which reflects the artist's love of Native American culture.
$195.00.
Photo by Jean Bernard

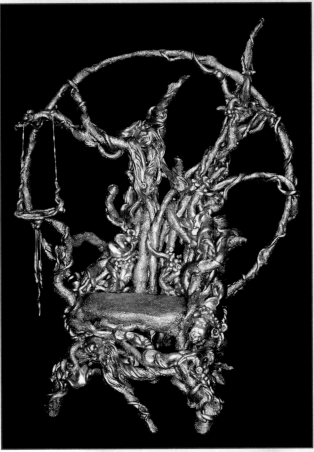

### Cheryl Brenner
Claude is a 28" bespectacled Sea Santa swaddled in fur trimmed coat and trousers. The net he clutches holds lots of shells and coral and a small boat is tucked under one arm. $300.00.
Photo by Larry Lauszus

### Deanna Brenner
Wendel is Deanna Brenner's 33" Old World Santa garbed in a coat and hat that was made from a vintage quilt and trimmed in mink. He has an armload of antique toys including a doll, bear, celluloid lamb, and drum. He also holds an antique tree with glass balls and glass bead garland. Wendel's mittens are made from leather and he wears hand-carved wooden shoes. $650.00.
Photo by Larry Lauszus

### Dru Esslinger
"Having been an elementary teacher for 30 years, 'Sh-h-h-h' is a part of my vocabulary!" Dru Esslinger denies wearing the type of hat with which she has topped her latest soft sculpture doll, but notes that with its entertainment industry look, the felt headpiece was a perfect fit. The 19" Sh-h-h poses in a tailored suit and leather shoes, also designed by Dru, on a removable stand. $300.00.
Photo by Dru Esslinger

### Lindy Evans
Marionette Workshop Santa is made of polymer clay and fabric and stands 6" tall, 2½" wide. Lindy sculpted the one-of-a-kind figure from tools made from piano wires — with lots of magnification! $300.00.
Photo by Geoffrey Carr

### Sherry Goshon
Echlin & the Enchanted Gourd is a one of a kind, very earthy 9" gourd doll perched on a throne. She reflects Sherry's gift of lyricism in the needle arts. $400.00.
Photo by Sherry Goshon

### Mary Ellen Frank
Sculpted of polyform, the media commissioned for this work, is a portrait doll of Mary Jo Hobbs, a master quilt maker from Juneau, Alaska. The doll wears a miniature reproduction of Hobbs' favorite dress while seated in a chair upholstered with fabric from one in her house and working on an embroidered photo reproduction on fabric of her quilt which won top honors in the local quilt show. The doll measures 10" x 7" x 8" with polyform head, hands, and lower arms, feet, and lower legs and fabric-stuffed body. She has Icelandic sheep hair. Commissioned by the subject.
Photo by Mary Ellen Frank

### Sherry Goshon

The 22" Take Time to Listen to YOUR Music is a new one-of-a-kind soft sculpture by Sherry Goshon. Boldly geometric in its black and white print, this doll has a strong sense of style — and purpose. $375.00.
Photo by Sherry Goshon

### Cheri Hiers

Cheri Hiers' 7" tall Oriental Faerie is a porcelain and polymer clay piece fitted with the wings of a small cicada. "She is one of my new clothed fairies, which is the direction I see some of my fairies going." Although her clothing is sculpted of clay, the gold-flecked red costume looks refined and delicate. Oriental Faerie has inset eyes, applied eyelashes, and viscose hair, and she lounges with a Panda friend. $375.00.
Photo by Cheri Hiers

### Kim Jelley

Kim's one-of-a-kind baby doll is sculpted of polymer clay, measures 19" long, and weighs 6½ pounds. She is adorned in a crocheted Christening outfit that was created specifically for the baby by Kim's sister-in-law, Virginia Anderson. $2,500.00 (sold).
Photo by Kim Jelley

### Kim Jelley

The artist's latest creations tell a tale of two sensibilities (see Kim's baby on page 153.) Bettie Page, Queen of Pin-Up, is a 9" hand-sculpted polymer clay portrait of the legendary model. "I sculpted her portrait because I have been a long-time fan of hers." Kim has actually been in contact with Page's agents to request permission to send a photo of her sculpt to her. Kim made the doll a removable leopard bikini and gave her hand-painted eyes and features. Not for sale.
Photo by Kim Jelley

### Gail Lackey

Moon Dandy was inspired by the automatons of the 1880s. Sculpted of polymer clay over wire armature, the 17" piece features antique fabrics and trims and glass eyes. This piece is in a private collection.
Photo by Gail Lackey

### Colleen Levitan

Colleen's 32" polymer clay portrait of Kate, a 20-something from Great Britain recreated in her 10-year-old image, illustrates the artist's ever-evolving intuitiveness in connecting with her subjects. Kate, an animal lover, is depicted holding a monkey, a kitten, and a puppy in her lap. "I didn't know she was an animal lover when I sculpted the piece, but I found out later from Kate's mother, so that worked out really well." $4,500.00.
Photo by Colleen Levitan

## Mary Ellen Lucas

Standing nearly 12" tall from bejeweled or feathered head-dresses to slippers, the Empress of China and the Black Widow are part of a new line of fantasy figures by Mary Ellen Lucas. The dolls boast the artist's continued commitment to using recycled materials: the Black Widow's sequins were given to Mary Ellen from ladies of Emmanuel Methodist Church in Ft. Mitchell, Kentucky; her gold spider web was a pin bought by the artist's late husband years ago; and the web was formerly a chapel veil. The pearl necklace worn by the Empress of China also came from the "church ladies"; the robe is made from old dance costumes; and the pearls in the headdress were once earrings. Not for sale.
Photo by Kathryn Witt

## Karen Morley

Dark beauty Maegen exemplifies Karen's artistry in the fashion doll repaint niche. Maegen has had all of her original paint and lashes removed and has been completely repainted using quality acrylic paints and sealers. She has newly applied and very soft, human hair lashes. Her nails and toenails have been painted and her breasts have been painted in natural detail. High gloss sealer enhances her eyes, nails, and lips, and a UV protectant matte finish has been applied. In private collection.
Photo by Karen Morley

## Linnea Polk

Wesley, Keeper of the Royal Silk Worms is Linnea's latest addition to a gallery of figures that includes trolls and her signature Flyhoppers™. Made of polymer clay, Wesley is clad in upholstery fabric and trimmed with assorted cords and beads. Each one-of-a-kind monkey comes with a short "bio." $85.00.
Photo by Linnea Polk

**Anna D. Puchalski**
Bug Tea Party is a wonderful example of the sense of diversion and duality that Anna brings to her original one-of-a-kind work. $190.00.
Photo by Anna D. Puchalski

**Anna D. Puchalski**
Waif is a ⅙ scale vinyl action figure by Toy2R designed by Anna. She has articulation at the head, shoulders, and hips, features rooted hair and fabric clothes, and comes with accessories. Item not yet priced.
Photo by Anna D. Puchalski

**Marilyn Radzat**
Rising Grace is 21" of iridescent ice-blue beauty. "The color of these tiles change as light is reflected upon them. They are a glass much like the ancient Roman glass that reflects gold and peach and pink according to the light." Marilyn created the pattern on either side of the tiles using turquoise sea glass she collected on deserted beaches near where she lives. Stunning both in detail and simplicity, Rising Grace is a blessing piece, a vision of rising energy, like grace. "I have studied with a Taoist master and she has given me permission to use these hand signatures, which are thousands of years old, in my artwork." $3,000.00.
Photo by John Chisholm

### Marilyn Radzat

As dark as Rising Grace is light is the ebony enchantress, Starry Starry Nights who sits upon a throne of mosaic mirrors, pondering the coming of the day. "She sits, completely relaxed, and given over to her memory of the night." Tiny Swarovski rhinestones, like stars fallen from the midnight sky, dot her headpiece and costume, reflecting a dance of light against the deep black of her costume. This piece measures approximately 16½" from the bottom of her chair to the top of her feathers. $2,400.00.
Photo by John Chisholm

### Monica Reo

This 36" porcelain beauty exquisitely crafted by Monica Reo is a combination of both French and English fashion. "My inspiration comes from the times of the French Consulate and First Empire (1799 – 1815) that was greatly influenced by the steady immigration of French refugee courtiers to London, changing English fashions from 1790 to 1830." Olivia, extravagantly garbed in a slate blue gown, is an English subject attending a masquerade ball at the French Court of Marseilles, 1814, during the exile of Napoleon. "Watching the movie, *The Count of Monte Christo*, had a big impact in creating Olivia." $4,800.00.
Photo by John Reo

### Mo'a Romig-Boyles

The 12" Princess Papillon was so named because the collar of her garment reminded her creator of the gentle curve of a butterfly wing. The base is a gourd and the doll's face, hair, hands, and base structure are sculpted of Aves Apoxie Sculpt. Mo'a covered the dress with fabric trims, painted dots and beads, and then crowned her piece with a charm detailed with beads. $575.00.
Photo by Mo'a Romig-Boyles

### Sue Sizemore

Alexandra is sweet as apple pie in her Victorian child's dress and stockinged feet. She stands 3', 4" tall and is made of knit fabric with needle-sculpted face. She has wired fingers and synthetic hair. A gold pendant necklace is a fitting adornment. $825.00.
Photo by Sue Sizemore

### Jamie Williamson

With her luminous German glass hazel eyes, Her Royal Highness is a regal vision in silver organza with antique lace and rhinestone trim, crowned with a headpiece of rhinestone and sheer teal underlay. The piece is part of a vignette that includes a hand-painted embossed backdrop, also made by Jamie, complete with ornate silver frame, a cut velvet cushion with tassel trim, and a footstool upholstered in raw silk with beaded ball fringe. $9,000.00.
Photo by Jamie Williamson

### Karen Williams Smith

Made of polymer clay and with painted eyes and Tibetan lamb hair, the 8" Marina Dawn is the first mermaid Karen has made that is fully sculpted under the tail. "I wanted this to be a real little girl in a mermaid costume so she has fully sculpted legs and feet under the tail costume." The shell and pearl are also sculpted and the base is beaded and trimmed with real starfish. "It was a challenge to figure out how to make the shell and pearl look like they were real. I ended up using several fingernail polishes to achieve that pretty translucent opalescence." Not for sale.
Photo by John G. Smith

### Lorna Miller-Sands

Just arrived at the nursery is Cara, a sweet-faced, realistic baby that measures 20" long. "I found a photo and was inspired by the subject's pouty expression." Cara is one of the artist's new, one-of-a-kind white babies. $2,395.00.
Photo by Barbara Stewart

### Marcia Dundore Wolter

Hina, Goddess of the Moon, features paperclay head, hands, and feet on a cloth body with wire armature. She is an acrobat trained at Cirque du Soleil where she portrays the goddess of the heavens, Hina, as she performs in the circle of the full moon. The light of the moon shines on the choppy sea below. She is reaching for the smaller ring above, which she will use to continue her act. "This piece was inspired by the lore and legend of the island of Maui." It also won first place for trueness of technique at the WOW! 2004 Doll Challenge sponsored by the Academy of American Doll Artists. $495.00.
Photo by Alan Love of Love's Photography

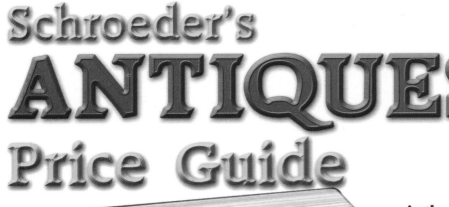

# For Catherine

Copyright © 1999 by John Wallace

First published in Great Britain in 1999 by Penguin Books Ltd.
First published in the United States by Holiday House, Inc. in 2000.
All Rights Reserved

First Edition

Printed in Hong Kong by Wing King Tong Co. Ltd.

Library of Congress Cataloging-in-Publication Data

Wallace, John, 1966-
Tiny Rabbit goes to a birthday party / John Wallace.
p.   cm.
Summary: Tiny Rabbit is worried about going to Blue Mouse's birthday
party because he has never been to a party before, but then he
finds himself enjoying the games and the food.
ISBN 0-8234-1489-2
[l. Parties—Fiction. 2. Birthdays—Fiction.
3. Rabbits—Fiction. 4. Animals—Fiction.] I. Title.
PZ7.W1567Ti   2000   99-25072
[E]—DC21   CIP

# TINY Rabbit

## Goes to a Birthday Party

## John Wallace

Holiday House / New York

A special letter had arrived in the mail for Tiny Rabbit. He opened it.
"It's an invitation to Blue Mouse's birthday party!" said Tiny Rabbit.
"Hooray!"

Tiny Rabbit was *so* excited. He'd never been to a party before. He phoned Pig to find out what happened at parties. Tiny Rabbit had a lot to do to get ready!

First, Tiny Rabbit needed to choose something to wear. He tried on his favorite outfits...

Fire bunny...

Doctor...

Bat bunny . . .

"I know!" said Tiny Rabbit. "I'll just go as myself."

Next, Tiny Rabbit had to find the perfect present. What would Blue Mouse *really* like?

A carrot?

A picture?

Some lettuce?

"I know!" said
Tiny Rabbit.

"I'll give him . . .

...this big cardboard box!"

Tiny Rabbit started to wrap up the box.

It was a bit
tricky . . .

and he got a
bit sticky . . .

but he managed
in the end.

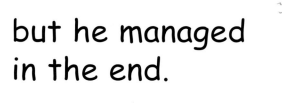

On the way to Blue Mouse's party,
Tiny Rabbit began thinking.

"What if I don't know anyone?
What if I don't like the food?
What if I want to go home?"

By the time he got to the party,
Tiny Rabbit was feeling a bit scared.
He wasn't sure he'd enjoy himself.
"I think I'll just stay
here and watch,"
thought Tiny Rabbit.

But then Blue Mouse saw Tiny Rabbit
and came over.
"Happy birthday," whispered Tiny
Rabbit, feeling very shy. "Here's
your present."

"Wow! Thank you," said Blue Mouse, and started to unwrap the big, mysterious present. "It's a box! I love it!" cried Blue Mouse.

Everyone started playing with the box.

They climbed
into it . . .

scrambled
through it ...

and hid
inside it.

Tiny Rabbit thought it looked like fun,
but didn't think he wanted to join in.

When the real games started,
Striped Cat held out his paw
and said, "Come on, Tiny Rabbit.
Come and play!"

Soon Tiny Rabbit stopped feeling shy and joined in.

Then it was time to eat. Tiny Rabbit
had a bit of everything, and even
tried some things he'd never
had before.

Striped Cat ate so much
that he fell off his chair.

Next, Blue Mouse had to make a wish while he blew out all the candles on his birthday cake. All his friends counted, "One . . . two . . . three . . . ." Whoosh!

Blue Mouse didn't blow quite hard enough, so Tiny Rabbit joined in to help. Tiny Rabbit really had to huff and puff, but he managed in the end.

All too soon it was the end of the
party. Tiny Rabbit had forgotten
how he'd felt when he first arrived,
and went home feeling very full
and very happy.

When he got home, Tiny Rabbit had
lots to do. It would be *his* birthday
in four weeks and two days, and he
had a birthday party to plan!